BTS

ICONS OF K-POP

BTS

ICONS OF K-POP
The Unofficial Biography

ADRIAN BESLEY

Michael O'Mara Books Limited

For Nora and Polly

First published in Great Britain in 2018 by
Michael O'Mara Books Limited
9 Lion Yard
Tremadoc Road
London SW4 7NQ

A CIP catalogue record for this book is available from the British Library.

Papers used by Michael O'Mara Books Limited are natural, recyclable products made from wood grown in sustainable forests. The manufacturing processes conform to the environmental regulations of the country of origin.

ISBN: 978-1-78243-968-4 in paperback print format
ISBN: 978-1-78243-970-7 in ebook format

1 3 5 7 9 10 8 6 4 2

Cover design by Ana Bjezancevic
Cover images: Jason LaVeris / FilmMagic / Getty Images (front), RB / Bauer-Griffin / GC Images / Getty Images (back)
Designed and typeset by Mark Bracey

Printed and bound by CPI Group (UK) Ltd, Croydon, CR0 4YY

Follow us on Twitter @OMaraBooks

www.mombooks.com

CONTENTS

INTRODUCTION

BANGTAN WORLD

When BTS topped the US Billboard album charts in May 2018, many people were left wondering who this band were and where they'd come from. On the face of it, the answer was simple: BTS are seven very talented boys from South Korea who make music that the whole world has come to love. But those who follow K-pop, especially ARMY, BTS's dedicated fans, know there's a whole lot more to it than that.

BTS are one of many K-pop groups, but what's remarkable about them is that they're a K-pop group unlike any other in the history of Korean entertainment culture. BTS are unique because they've succeeded without the backing of a major music company, the members of the group contribute to the writing and production of their own songs and, most notably, they're not afraid to talk about their aspirations and their anxieties, and to be the voice of their generation.

This book charts the rise of BTS. From seven boys with seven dreams to one superstar group of young men who achieved a shared vision of global success, *BTS: Icons of K-Pop* will demonstrate just how they reached such remarkable heights, all while singing and rapping in a language many probably don't understand. The songs are an irresistible combination of catchy and emotional, and the dances are simply awe-inspiring. The book will also look at the background to BTS's music, detail exactly what it's like to see BTS live and which big names BTS have met along the way. And then, of course, there are the haircuts and the clothes. Welcome to the world of Bangtan!

The book will also look at the band's incredible fan base. ARMY are one of the most – if not *the* most – informed, dedicated and unified fandoms in the world. Not only are they vociferous about their love for the group, but they translate lyrics and interviews, have helped BTS win awards and have created an online community that reflects the ideals of the group themselves. Their story is part of BTS's story, and neither would be the same without the other.

BTS are also known for their huge online presence, one of the highlights being their Bangtan bombs. These short videos are full of shared jokes or offer brilliant insights into the life and times of BTS, and a number of these are recorded in these pages. At the end of the book you'll also find a glossary that explains some useful Korean words and K-pop terms.

The group's journey hasn't been easy, and each and every member has had to work incredibly hard. As teenage trainees from ordinary backgrounds they rehearsed until they were note- and step-perfect. That determination and dedication is still evident today and this book is also about their individual personalities, their friendships, their moments of self-doubt and their elation at their achievements.

BTS have millions of fans all over the globe and have achieved so many of their goals. They've come a long way and who knows how much further they have to go, but whatever the future holds, the story of how they became icons of not just K-pop but the world is a fascinating one. I hope you enjoy seeing it told for the first time.

Adrian Besley

BEGINNINGS

Have you ever seen anything like BTS before? Those choreographed moves; rappers and singers in the same group? Boys living and training together for years before their first performance? Appearing on a constant stream of music shows or taking on strange and silly challenges on television? If you've followed K-pop any time in the last ten years, then perhaps you have – even if no group has done those things quite like BTS.

The story of BTS can't be told without reference to the culture and traditions of K-pop. While they are now an international phenomenon, they were once a group of boys just happy to make music; recording their first song and performing on Korean television felt like the ultimate achievement. They had grown up with K-pop and understood the particular expectations, hardships and trials of the idol life. That they attempted this, succeeded against all the odds and pushed the boundaries of K-pop is just one aspect of the amazing nature of this group.

What we call K-pop began in 1992. It can be dated to the appearance of Seo Taiji and Boys on a TV talent show where they performed their single 'Nan Arayo' ('I Know'). They came last in the talent show, but their single, an innovative fusion of American and Korean pop, soon topped the country's charts – for seventeen weeks. Seo Taiji and Boys

Seo Taiji and Boys would inspire a host of new groups eager to give US rock, pop, R&B and especially 1990s hip-hop a unique Korean flavour.

(who years later invited BTS to appear at their reunion) would inspire a host of new groups eager to create Korean music influenced by US rock, pop, R&B and especially 1990s hip-hop.

Despite the US influence, Korean pop music would establish its own distinct characteristics. The conservative moral code of Korean society holds sway, ensuring that songs with references to sex, drugs and alcohol are banned from radio and television, and there is almost no tradition of questioning society or raising political issues in music. Artists are expected to remain charming and innocent at all times.

Then there is Korean television, which is watched by millions and vital to the success of K-pop acts. Music shows proliferate, with *Inkigayo*, *Music Core*, *Music Bank*, *M Countdown*, *Show Champion* and *The Show Choice* ensuring there is a pop programme on TV most days of the week. The fact that the shows usually feature 'live' acts instead of music videos ensures that performance is a prized aspect of K-pop. On-point choreography, stage presence, stunning outfits and good looks are essential.

Acts will try to feature their 'debut' (first) or 'comeback' (new) songs on these shows, and each awards a weekly trophy based on various permutations of chart position, downloads and viewers' votes. These trophies are fiercely contested, with the ultimate achievement being a clean sweep of victories across all shows, BTS's 'DNA' being one of only four songs ever to do this.

K-pop artists are also expected to take their place, as a group or individually, alongside comedians, actors and other celebrities on the nation's incredibly popular variety shows. These sometimes involve interviews and performances, but more often focus on amusing challenges that highlight artists' characters, skills and humour. BTS made a great early impression with appearances on *Knowing Bros* and *Weekly Idol*, and went on to have their own variety shows in *Rookie King*, *Run BTS!* and *BTS Gayo*. There are even regular televised Idol Games, a mini-Olympics in which K-pop artists compete against each other in various sports, BTS being particularly strong in the 4 × 400 metre relay.

Having established themselves, K-pop artists eagerly await the awards season that spans the New Year period. There are many ceremonies, but the most prestigious are the Golden Disc Awards, the Melon Music Awards (MMAs), Mnet Asian Music Awards (MAMAs) and the Seoul Music Awards. These offer *bonsangs* or prizes given to a number of high-achieving acts, but every artist ultimately craves a *daesang*, the top prize given for the artist of the year and, depending on the ceremony, sometimes for the song and album of the year, too.

With such exposure, K-pop artists are expected to be singers and dancers, look great and show their personality. This doesn't happen naturally. Remember the pioneering Seo Taiji and Boys? When they split in 1996, Yang Hyun-suk, one of the 'Boys', set up YG Entertainment to create, produce and manage K-pop groups. Around the same time and with the same aims, SM Entertainment and JYP Entertainment were formed. The 'Big Three', as they came to be known, would end up dominating K-pop, devising a conveyor-belt process that produced successful artists and groups who are known as idols.

The process begins with the companies hosting fiercely competitive auditions and scouring talent shows in search of potential idols. The successful young artists, often in their early teens or even younger, are

The successful young artists, often in their early teens or even younger, are contracted as trainees and live in dormitories with other hopefuls. Together they face a gruelling boot camp of dancing, singing and exercise.

contracted as trainees and live in dormitories with other hopefuls. Together they face a gruelling boot camp of dancing, singing, exercise, diet regimes, and English and Japanese lessons, as well as tuition on how to perform on TV and conduct themselves in public. On top of all that, they still have to do their schoolwork!

The company will put their trainees into groups or select them as solo artists, sometimes swapping them around or terminating their contracts if they don't make the grade or fit the particular requirements. K-pop groups often have more members than their Western equivalents, because they try to offer fans a complete package of skills. They have specialist rappers, vocalists, dancers and even 'visuals' – members included for their looks and stage presence. The company provides the name, image, choreography and songs, usually with little input from the group.

Common to nearly every K-pop group is a leader, who is often the eldest, although that isn't the case with BTS's RM. When they appear in public or collect awards, they act as the spokesperson and are also the go-between, taking instructions from the company and passing them on to the other members. The group will also have a *maknae*, the name given to the youngest member. In BTS that's Jungkook. The *maknae* is like the baby of the family, cute and adorable. Often extremely talented and beautiful, they are very much the pride of each group.

The launch of the act, usually on one of the weekly music shows, is known as their 'debut stage'. This is a massive moment for new groups. The company will have been preparing the ground for months, releasing teaser photographs of members, setting up social media accounts, posting preview performances and even starting a fan club. The passion of K-pop fans is an essential element in sustaining a successful act. Interaction with fans through social media and fan meets can quickly garner the most dedicated and loyal support. These fans are often given an official name by the group, have their own forums and create an incredible atmosphere at concerts. The group Twice named their fan club Once, BIGBANG have VIP and, of course, BTS have ARMY.

K-pop fans have devised ingenious ways of interacting with their idols. Not content with simple screaming and wild applause (although that happens), they hold up light sticks in the group's colour, sometimes in coordinated waves, produce massive banners of support and perform fan chants over the intros and breaks or as a reply to choruses.

If a new group can negotiate a successful debut and build a fan base, they will have a chance of a 'comeback'. This doesn't mean they remain dormant for a time or even necessarily have a break; it's just the term used for the launch of a new single or album and its promotion on the weekly shows. Once again previewed and teased beforehand, the comeback often has a new 'concept': a subtle or even a major change in image or sound.

Once established, the K-pop act is perfectly placed to ride a wave – the Korean wave known as *hallyu*. Korean culture has been growing in global prominence over the past decade. From television drama to cosmetics and especially pop music, South Korean exports have become fashionable and popular from Japan to the USA. Psy's hit 'Gangnam

Style' is the obvious example, but BIGBANG, EXO and others have also made inroads into the US Billboard charts.

To get this far requires a lot of investment, influence and know-how from the entertainment company. Success breeds success and the Big Three have come to dominate and even control the K-pop industry. Some groups had proved it is possible to get a small foothold in the business, but to make it as international idols? That's surely a dream too far. It would take someone with great experience, a little luck and a willingness to stretch K-pop's rules and traditions. Enter Bang Si-hyuk.

Bang Si-hyuk was a successful composer and producer with Big Three company JYP. He had established a reputation as a hit-maker with groups such as g.o.d and Wonder Girls, earning his nickname 'Hitman'. In 2005, he left JYP to set up his own entertainment company, named Big Hit. He had some success with mixed-gender group 8Eight, and with 2AM, and then in 2010 he came up with a plan to launch a rap act. This plan was the seed that would grow into a K-pop colossus: BTS.

Kim Namjoon, soon to be named Rap Monster (later shortened to RM), had joined Big Hit as a solo rapper in 2010. He had been rapping in the underground scene, a more rebellious arena than idol K-pop where artists can act independently but perform to comparatively small crowds. As the idea of a rap act took root in the mind of Bang Si-hyuk, he moved RM into an embryonic group with other underground rappers, including Kidoh (who ended up in idol group Topp Dogg), Iron and Supreme Boi, which was further expanded with the arrival of Min Yoongi (Suga).

Around the end of 2011, Hitman Bang changed the direction of the group to pursue

> As the idea of a group took root, Bang Si-hyuk moved RM into an embryonic group with other underground rappers.

a less rap-focused, more mainstream sound with vocalists as well as rappers. Dance prodigy Jung Hoseok (J-Hope), who had joined the company the previous year, was one possible singer (he would only later become a rapper). Some of the rappers left, unhappy with this new approach. Supreme Boi stayed at Big Hit, but as a songwriter and producer. He would become an integral part of BTS – in many ways the eighth Bangtan Boy. Pdogg, a Big Hit producer (and still an important member of the BTS production team), was charged with putting this group together. He had around thirty trainees at Big Hit and he would watch, record and assess them, put them into teams and give them assignments.

By early 2012, Jungkook, Taehyung (V) and then Seokjin (Jin) had auditioned and joined the Big Hit team. However, the line-up was still not fixed. Other trainees in the mix included Jeong In-seong and Seung-Jun, who now line up with idol group KNK, and Boys Republic member Suwoong. For all these guys, undergoing the arduous trainee hardships and homesickness, the future was still uncertain: they might not be selected for the group and even then they might have a long wait before they debuted.

In the early summer of 2012, Jimin, the last member of the group to join, signed with Big Hit. BTS were finally taking shape, with four making up what K-pop fans call the 'rap line' (Kidoh would leave later in the year) and four on the 'vocal line'. This proposed idol group even had a name. Big Kids and Young Nation were among those considered, but Bangtan Sonyeondan, which translates to Bulletproof Boy Scouts, was the preferred option – at least by the Big Hit supremo, whose opinion counted most.

Bang Si-hyuk had now assembled and selected his group. He had a leader in Rap Monster, the first of them to join Big Hit, who was intelligent and articulate, with the bonus of being fluent in English; a main dancer, J-Hope, who was a national dance competition-winner; and a *maknae* in Jungkook, who could have signed with one of the Big Three. The others had shown they were prepared to put in the necessary hours of hard work and showed real promise. Most of all, they were a completely charming group of boys, who seemed to bring out the best in each other.

Bang Si-hyuk had now assembled and selected his group. He had a leader who was intelligent and articulate, a main dancer who was a national dance competition-winner, and a *maknae* who could have signed with one of the Big Three.

Bang Si-hyuk had a vision for his new group. He had given them a name that showed they would fight the prejudices and hardships experienced by their generation. They would speak out for teens and twenty-somethings. In order for this to work, he loosened some of the shackles of K-pop. He gave the group, starting with the rap line, an opportunity to contribute to the lyrics. He encouraged them to speak freely about issues that affect young people and enabled them, through every social media channel available, to become as close to their fans as possible.

The task for Bangtan Sonyeondan (many would soon be calling them BTS) appeared enormous. Their company had very little money with which to back them and break the supremacy of SM Entertainment's EXO and Girls' Generation or YG's BIGBANG and G-Dragon. Their songs were based around 1990s-style US rap that was losing popularity in Korea and the rebellious attitude of their songs was already raising eyebrows. The group had a mountain to climb before they even got started. As 2013 approached, they prepared to take their first steps up that mountain.

TWO

WE ARE BULLETPROOF

D o you remember where you were on 13 June 2013? It was a Thursday and you were probably tucked up in bed dreaming but, as you slept, on the other side of the world, in Seoul, South Korea, seven guys were hitting the stage on a TV music show. BTS was happening.

One day, 13 June will be an international holiday, but let's rewind a little … Out in Korea, intriguing teasers had been emerging for some time about a fresh new group. With his extensive experience in the K-pop business, Big Hit Entertainment CEO Bang Si-hyuk knew just how to build excitement for a new act. Back in 2012, Big Hit had launched a blog that announced the impending arrival of Bangtan Sonyeondan, introduced the band members and showcased their photos to those early followers. The word was out: Big Hit had an idol group in the making.

On 17 December 2012, a YouTube account was created as the first bit of BTS content was aired: a video of original member Rap Monster's version of Kanye West's 'Power'. This was soon followed by another RM rap, 'Let's Introduce BANGTAN ROOM'. These first two videos are

> Word was out: Big Hit had an idol group in the making.

still up on YouTube – watch the latter for a very cool cameo from Jin. And then came a Christmas present, as the Big Hit supremo Bang Si-hyuk, using his nickname Hitman Bang, introduced 'A Typical Trainee's Christmas'. This half a song, with a self-edited video, was a teaser for his next Big Hit auditions. Once again, Rap Mon takes the mic, but this time Jin and Suga, who had been recruited at a previous audition, take a turn.

On watching the video, it's apparent that these boys aren't playing the usual game. Here's a group who aren't afraid to answer back to their record company; a group who will reveal exactly how life is for the idol in training. While Jin sweetly covers the opening of the 1984 Wham! hit 'Last Christmas', the rap line complains of a lonely Christmas of endless practice and even asks how the group are supposed to write love songs when they are forbidden girlfriends.

On the same day the YouTube account had been created, BTS had entered the Twittersphere with the promise that the lead-up to their debut would be full of fun exploits. Who would have thought that in just a few years they would dominate Twitter! It was almost 2013 and BTS were out there – if you were a K-pop fan and were paying attention.

In January 2013 a new song found its way on to YouTube. A simply but artfully shot film employing a black background and extreme close-ups showed RM, Suga and Jin rapping. 'School of Tears' used the beats and flow of Kendrick Lamar's 'Swimming Pools', but the trio sang their own very personal lyrics. They talked of the dark side of school life: the bullying, and the fears of those who don't protect the bullied in case the same thing happens to them. Rap Mon is sporting the new dreadlocks he had put in for New Year (he takes them out at the end of January) and he was reminded of this video in September

2016 when the others surprised him by playing it as part of his birthday celebrations.

Through the early months of the year, BTS members regularly sat down in the studio to record their diary entries. In these vlogs they were usually alone on screen, although we later learned that, of course, other group members were sometimes out of shot, pulling faces and teasing them. Frank and open, funny and sensitive, BTS showed they were ready to talk to their fans about anything – and that included their insecurities and their anxieties.

> They were ready to talk to their fans about anything – and that included their insecurities and their anxieties.

In one of his videos, RM tells us that he's upset to have been told that Big Hit doesn't believe he'll make it as a full-on solo rapper. On 8 January, he complains that he's unable to come up with rap lines – he's exhausted, cold, wants to go home and isn't feeling inspired – but he knows the company expects him to come up with something. Jin, in his vlog, tells of being away from home and having to look after himself, and we can see the first signs of his interest in cooking. Then an adorably shy Jimin appears to do his first vlog and, having teased the others while they recorded theirs, can't think of anything to say.

In early February, Jungkook made his first log entry. It's his middle-school graduation day and he says he knows he should be happy but, as the *maknae* (the youngest in the group, still only fifteen years old), he expresses just how homesick he feels – it's a heartbreaking entry. J-Hope is more upbeat as he states his pre-debut goals of making his rapping cooler and his dancing more professional, but throughout the early entries, often recorded late at night or in the early hours of the morning after a long day's work, the boys are very tired, quite shy and rather overwhelmed by the position they find themselves in.

The release of the joyous 'Graduation Song' video was therefore very welcome. Jungkook, Jimin and J-Hope stepped forward to take their turn in the limelight. And boy did they shine – in and out of their school uniforms! Their snappy light-rap song covered Snoop Dogg, Wiz Khalifa and Bruno Mars' 'Young, Wild & Free'. The witty and upbeat replacement lyrics, written by J-Hope and producer Supreme Boi, celebrated the end of school and the freedoms of adult life. Even then, though, debut was on their mind – in one line, J-Hope even asks the boss if debuting is really meant to be this tough. This song, along with the vlogs, helped generate interest – it was vital that they had built a following before their first public appearance.

The Lunar New Year is a big deal in Korea. In 2013 it fell on 10 February. Like Thanksgiving in the US, it's traditional to spend time with your family and it couldn't have come at a better time for seven boys who had worked themselves into the ground. Having gone home, seen their families, slept and eaten well for a couple of days, they returned refreshed. Their debut was finally in sight and this came across in their vlogs: they were excited and all rededicated themselves to the BTS cause. Hard work was the mantra: we will work even harder to build a better Bangtan!

Throughout April and May, the exhausted Bangtan Boys appeared, discussing final choreography practices for their debut, recording tracks for their single album and filming their music video. It was getting closer! In his 14 May vlog, RM marked the shooting of his first ever music video as the end of their long trainee life. Then, a few days later, they all appeared together for the first time in a group vlog, talking about their video filming and reading out support messages from fans, adding that, although it was still nearly a month away, this would be the last vlog before their debut.

Okay. They all appeared together, but attentive ARMY will know there was one key member missing. Taehyung, known as V, was notable for his absence throughout the vlogs and videos. V had been part of BTS for over two years, training, singing and dancing with the others, but he was never announced as a member; he wasn't able to post a vlog and the others couldn't mention him. Poor V! He was the secret weapon and, in a clever play by Big Hit, knowledge of his existence was held back for maximum effect.

Debut is make or break time for K-pop groups and the pressure was building. For some this is the satisfying culmination of three years of unrelenting hard work; for others it is simply incredibly nerve-racking, but as the big day approached it was the group's spirit and togetherness that saw them through.

On 21 May 2013, a countdown-to-debut clock was revealed on the website and the debut trailer released. It was a forty-five-second, black-and-white montage of the members' names and a series of hard-hitting slogans that formed into a firing revolver. Then, on 2 June, preview photos on the BTS page of the Big Hit website and Facebook gave us the first pictures of Taehyung, looking suitably moody with shaggy, cropped blond hair. Big Hit's plan seemed to have worked and, by debut day, less than two weeks later, V already had five fan clubs of his own!

At the bottom of the home page, next to the countdown clock, was a simple tease asking: who's next? The answer came the very next day in the shape of Jin, Jimin and Jungkook – which really got K-popsters chattering. Finally, a day after that, came the rap line. Fans were already familiar with RM, J-Hope and Suga through the tracks, videos and vlogs, but this was showtime – and they looked good!

All the pictures showed the members in their hip-hop and bad-boy gear: all leathers and logos, skate wear and sports clothes. J-Hope was in a studded mask; RM had shades, a medallion and dollar-sign cane; Suga wielded a skateboard; Jungkook wore a hockey mask and gold hand-bone jewellery; Jimin was cute in his basketball kit; Jin looked every bit the b-boy in his backwards baseball cap and baggy shorts; and V posed in his black leather like the coolest kid in school. It was a look we would see again.

The training had finished for now. The teasers had been shown. The countdown was over. It was time. BTS, meet the world ... World, meet BTS. Their debut showcase took place on 12 June at the Ilchi Art Hall in Cheongdam-dong, in the Gangnam area of the city. But it was the following day that counted, when the band appeared live on stage for the first time on the TV shows *M Countdown* and *Music Bank*.

> The training had finished for now. The teasers had been shown. The countdown was over. It was time. BTS, meet the world ... World, meet BTS.

You can still watch the BTS debut-day video on YouTube and see seven unbelievably young Bangtan Boys about to face the public in a live premiere showcase. They are understandably nervous, hiding their anxieties by practising their routines one last time, teasing each other or just sitting quietly, each one a demonstration of just how dedicated these boys were. As V says, 'We only have one chance!'

Of course, once they were up on stage, throwing themselves into 'No More Dream', they were sharp and they were slick. Afterwards, ever the perfectionist, Jin was in tears after the microphone pack had made his trousers slip down, but his bandmates consoled him. He had no time to dwell on it as they were soon due back on stage for their other promoted song, 'We Are Bulletproof Pt. 2'.

On the YouTube clip, you can see by their faces when they had finished the day's performances that they'd given their all, but they knew they'd nailed it. Their energy, rap style and dance moves, especially Jungkook's hat flick and Jimin's abs flash, had attracted attention. Like most debuting groups, BTS had set up a forum known as a 'fan café' – this had already swollen to 55,000 members.

For three years they had dreamed of the moment when they would take to the stage, so it was no wonder they had felt so nervous. They all said that when they finished and heard the cheers they were close to tears – V even confessed he actually cried. They were proud but admitted to having made mistakes and RM noted how heavy his legs felt on stage compared to the practice sessions, but they also knew that they had already learned so much over this brief debut period.

In the meantime, their first music video, 'No More Dream', had been released the day before debut. The hip-hop idol theme and attitude matched their teaser pictures and debut performances, and the scenario was one of upheaval and rebellion, where the group, sporting plenty of black and white, drive – and crash – the school bus, BMX riders roam the streets and a refashioned classroom has a skate ramp and walls covered in BTS graffiti.

The choreography is very hip-hop, with a lot of low crouches, hip thrusts and lightning-fast pointing, and, helped by sharp editing, it keeps all the energy of the live performance. Those who saw the debut shows would have recognized Jungkook carrying Jimin as he runs horizontally across the backs of the others and, of course, the Jimin abs-flashes that sent the live audience into meltdown.

This track would feature on *2 Cool 4 Skool*, the first BTS CD, which

BANGTAN BOMB

VJ [THE FIRST BANGTAN BOMB]

On 19 June 2013, Bangtan TV posted a thirty-second video on YouTube. It showed Jungkook filming Jimin, and in the corner was a small logo: a cartoon BTS bomb. This was the first of many bombs – bite-sized videos of behind-the-scenes footage, challenges or just the boys acting cute or messing around. They last for anything from twenty seconds to two minutes and give fans a fascinating insight into BTS away from the stage.

was released on their debut day, 12 June 2013, and came in a stylish black-and-gold package. An attached photobook featured some glossy images similar to those revealed in the teasers, lyrics (in Korean), a postcard and a flyer advertising the next Big Hit auditions. This 'single album' with seven tracks would be the first of a trilogy of releases that explored themes of not being ground down by the school system, having pride in yourself and facing the trials of being young.

> BTS would be relevant and show they shared the aspirations and anxieties of their generation.

In this short-play album, RM declares the group's intention to talk to teens and twenty-somethings. This was what would set them apart from most other K-pop groups. BTS would be relevant and show they shared the aspirations and anxieties of their generation.

The album proper starts as 'We Are Bulletproof

Pt. 2' sets out the band's stall as a group who could rap better than idol bands and were as authentic as any Korean underground rapper. Next comes 'Skit: Circle Room Talk' (a skit is essentially members chatting – a feature of US hip-hop albums from De La Soul to Eminem), and it gave the boys a chance to discuss their ideas and the themes of the album before diving straight into 'No More Dream', their debut single and the key track on the record. If the BTS mission statement was to speak to and for teens and twenty-somethings, then this went straight to the heart of the matter – it is assertive, heavy on the attitude and catchy as hell.

RM's opening lyrics announced the group to the world and from the resonant twang of the double bass, through Suga's sarcastic lines about the big house, big cars and big rings he wants, to the la-la-la singalong (the first of many), the sound was big, the beat kept pumping and the melodic hooks kept coming. Meanwhile, the rap line took the spotlight, working around the chant, which asks the listener about their dream. The lyrics spoke passionately of a frustration and anger that young people don't dream and are unable to break out from the mundane lives plotted for them by their parents and society.

After the brief 'Interlude' (a tune RM liked so much he used it in 'Monterlude' on his mixtape), we are into 'I Like It' – and, what do you know, it's a pop song! Okay, there was still some rapping, but Jungkook and Jin had put down some sweet melodies in a song about seeing photos of an ex-girlfriend on social media. The album rounded off with the light-hearted outro 'Circle Room Cypher' (a cypher being a hip-hop term for a freestyle rap session). However, those who bought the CD were treated to two extra tracks: 'On the Start Line', delivered by RM, and 'Road/Path', featuring the whole crew. Both of these recalled the hardships of their trainee years, what they would be doing if they were not Bangtan and the strength they had gained from being together.

The debut period continued through the rest of June and July as the boys promoted their album via radio and TV broadcasts and through fan meets. There was one further notable milestone, though. On 9 July, on the BTS fan café, they announced a name for their fan club. From this time on, their fans would be called ARMY, an acronym for 'Adorable Representative MC for Youth'. They explained that an army needs its bulletproof armour, so the boys and their fans would always be bound together. BTS fans took to the name immediately – they had a cause to believe in and were now on the march.

After nearly fifty frenetic days, BTS's debut was finally over. They had not been a sensation – lots of people had dismissed them as just another hip-hop group, having taken against their rebellious image and anti-conservative lyrics, or had slated their chances of success because they weren't a Big Three group. But they had established a group ethic, an image, a self-belief and, most importantly, a fan base that already stretched from Korea and elsewhere in Asia, as far as the Americas, Europe and the Middle East. And there was more to come.

After their goodbye stage, which marks the end of a debut, heartfelt handwritten notes from all seven members of BTS appeared on their fan café. The band revealed how they felt when they set off on a journey without knowing the route or the destination. They described their

> From this time on their fans would be called ARMY, an acronym for 'Adorable Representative MC for Youth'. They explained that an army needs its bulletproof armour, so the boys and their fans would always be bound together.

debut as a whirlwind experience and said that although their training prepared them well for that experience, they knew they had so much more to offer. They were all overcome with gratitude for the support of the fans they had met in person and the fans whose messages they had read. Above everything, they said, this was what gave them the strength to enter the next stage of their career with confidence and optimism.

THREE

ROOKIE KINGS

They had debuted. The moment they had been dreaming of for so long had come and gone, but for the Bangtan Boys there was no let-up. There were fan meets, radio shows and dance practices to attend – and new tracks to record. It was a rollercoaster ride and they were hurtling along at full speed. Everybody needed to hold tight.

Within a few weeks of their goodbye stage, with *2 Cool 4 Skool* having reached number five in the South Korean album chart, BTS were recording new tracks. The Big Hit Entertainment countdown clock made its return on their website, along with a new trailer, released on 27 August 2013. In the trailer, BTS-branded trainers, a ring, mic and beatbox fall in slow motion as RM takes up the story where 'No More Dream' left off. Over a solemn backing track, he spells it out in English: it's time to live your own life, make your own decisions, now, before it's too late. As the beat kicks in, RM raps in his native tongue until the falling BTS items crash through glass.

A week later, there was more. A concept trailer saw the group, dressed in an all-black uniform of short-sleeved shirts, shorts and long BTS socks, surrounded and assassinated, one by one, by armed police. The idols lie fallen, until RM, who has sneakily escaped, returns to rouse them. Galvanized, they rip off their black shirts to reveal white, sleeveless tees. The dancing is fast and intense. They had clearly taken things up a level since the debut, with unbelievable popping and flawless synchronicity. It's a dance that's still ranked among their best ever.

Through their vlogs and tweets, the boys revealed not only the return of pre-debut nerves that had been lost in the adrenaline rush of their first performance, but also an expectation that they would all up their game. Could they? The answer is 'N.O', a track released on 10 September 2013.

> They had clearly taken things up a level since the debut ... It's a dance that's still ranked among their best ever.

The video for 'N.O' finds them in a chilling, dystopian school, where uniformed, drugged and soulless students take lessons under armed guard. As Jungkook leads a schoolroom rebellion, the video cuts to a bright, white studio and an outdoor scene with giant stone hands, where the dance action takes over. The choreography dials down the relentless energy and focuses on the emotional story, although there are still some stunning moves, not least when Jimin, so often teased for being the shortest, plays the hero. Jumping down from the back of the set, he executes an acrobatic mid-air spin and kick that lays low all of the oppressive police goons with one blow.

Most of all, though, the video celebrated the look of the group – collectively and individually. The new concept found them ditching the black for an angelic white, although, with V's distinctive faith chain, Suga's bandana and RM still in his shades, there was still plenty of bling and hip-hop style. The boys' hair had also changed: most noticeable was Jimin's new, smooth-as-silk coconut bowl, Suga had gone chocolate brown and curly, and V's hair was lighter with a purple tint.

Throughout September they were back promoting the new singles

'N.O' and 'Rise of Bangtan'. The K-pop world is ridiculously competitive and BTS needed to work hard to build a following. They did this through hosting fan meetings in Korea, posting on social media, through the Bangtan bombs on YouTube, and most importantly by appearing on the weekly television music shows where record sales, streams and viewers' votes all contributed to a show winner.

Though they were not yet in a position to compete with the massively popular and heavily promoted K-pop acts such as G-Dragon, BTS were getting noticed. On the *Music Bank* TV show, one performance gave fans an unexpected treat. As the boys tear their uniforms off to reveal their white tees, RM and Jimin, giving their all, accidentally rip half their T-shirts off as well. You can still relive the excitement – search YouTube for 'Rap Mon and Jimin ripping their shirts'.

The new ten-track album – the second of what will become their school trilogy – titled *O!RUL8,2?* (meaning, of course, 'Oh! Are you late, too?') was released on 11 September 2013. The CD package included a poster and a booklet featuring photoshoots from the new concept as well as two photo cards and a cartoon biography of BTS members.

RM's first trailer turned out to be the album intro and led logically into 'N.O', the promoted single. The lyrics, as the video suggested, once again zeroed in on school. 'N.O' (which also stands for 'No Offence') is a refusal to conform to parents' educational expectations. It expands on the themes of 'No More Dream' by addressing the intense pressures and relentless routines imposed upon students, especially in South Korea. Can you be happy just being a 'studying machine'? The message was that there are other options open to you: don't leave the pursuit of your dreams until it is too late.

> The message was ... don't leave the pursuit of your dreams until it is too late.

The music behind the message begins with a stirring orchestral sound, before letting the beat take over and the rapping and singing come to the fore. The lines are shared out pretty evenly among the group, with Jungkook, growing into his Golden *Maknae* nickname, even taking a rap turn.

Next up is 'We On'. This is a real gem with some very cool (and fast) understated rhymes in the rap line, contrasting with the sweetest of melodies from Jungkook and Jimin. The song is a proud answer to the haters who dissed BTS but sought their attention now they'd debuted. The skit 'R U Happy Now?' that follows is a short chat where the band talk of how tired they are, but also how content they are with where they are.

'If I Ruled the World' takes the rap line into their wildest dreams of fame, success and confidence (dreams that are now rapidly coming true!) with a catchy chorus, enhanced by one of the first examples of V's delicious, velvet-voiced melodies. This track is followed by the contrasting 'Coffee', a teenage break-up song, in which the sweet taste of the caramel macchiato they shared contrasts with the bitterness of the Americano now drunk alone. Clever, eh?

'Cypher Pt. 1' is their first serious rap-off (after the previous album's jokey attempt). It's fun, assertive and certainly proves they can bust some rhymes, skills which they continue to put to good use in 'Rise of Bangtan' (sometimes called 'Attack on Bangtan', a joke referencing the popular Japanese manga series *Attack on Titan*). A live favourite, so upbeat and full of energy, it's another BTS 'la-la-la' song.

'Paldogangsan', one of the first songs recorded by an early BTS back in August 2011, is better known as 'Satoori Rap'. *Satoori* are Korean dialects and this is a rap battle between the different dialects of Suga and J-Hope, with RM intervening in a standard Seoul dialect. On stage, the group had fun pitching a team from the East (Gyeongsan) against one from the West (Jeolla and Seoul).

After all that rap, it's only fair that the vocal line has the final say. 'Outro: Luv in Skool' might only last a minute and a half, but it is beautifully sung and its high number of views on YouTube has surely been boosted by those repeatedly listening to the song's (and album's) final words: Jungkook is asking you for a date!

> Jungkook is asking you for a date!

The Korean public love their television variety shows. Watching celebrities play games, attempt dances or try to complete absurd challenges is a national pastime. Of course, being a rookie group, it wasn't easy for BTS to get invited on such a show – so why not make a variety show themselves? South Korean broadcaster SBS's MTV channel had already had hits with the group Block B on *Match Up* and VIXX on *Plan V Diary*, but BTS were about to take the format and run with it.

Rookie King: Channel Bangtan, which appeared on South Korean music channel SBS MTV, was a parody of all the most successful Korean shows and it was very, very funny. Over eight fifty-minute episodes, BTS won the hearts of thousands more fans with their humour, easy-going nature and group friendship. The episodes are well worth watching online: from the first sketch, in which the boys dress in blue *hanboks* (traditional tunics) through to their version of *X-Man* (another popular South Korean game show), where one member is secretly selected to lose games (go on, guess who!), there's endless comedy and some great insight into the chemistry of BTS.

In between, there were some moments that reached mythic status. Episode one featured a hidden camera prank which saw each of the boys secretly filmed as a pretty young girl (an actress) entered their elevator in tears and pressed the button to every floor. Their reactions, from J-Hope's embarrassment at being caught dancing to Jin's touching concern, are all fascinating. And then there's the 'Open Your Heart' segment, which showed the boys screaming their most bitter complaints and confessions from a rooftop platform – including Suga revealing he stole Jungkook's underwear!

O!RUL8,2? went to number four in the Korean charts and 'N.O' was a modest success, reaching number ninety-two, which is an improvement on 'No More Dream', but these were still challenging times for the group. Yes they had debuted well and had had some television exposure, but the K-pop world is incredibly competitive and many were critical of their rap style, their rebellious lyrics and a hip-hop sound that some thought dated. Furthermore, to stay at the top required major financial backing, which Big Hit were struggling to find. The pressure to keep on going was huge.

Many other talented K-pop groups hadn't been able to live with this kind of pressure and it's no surprise that around this time there were rumours that BTS were considering disbanding. Imagine all of the amazing stuff we would have missed out on! It was ARMY that prevented them quitting. Their messages of love and support, and the enthusiastic attendance at fan meets, kept the boys going through the hard times.

The November 2013 Melon Music Awards came as a fabulous boost, then, as BTS won Best New Artist. If the boys had had one dream when they debuted in June, it was to win this prestigious rookie award, which is based on digital sales, judges' scores and online votes. This was the recognition they were hoping for, but they couldn't

> ARMY's messages of love and support, and the enthusiastic attendance at fan meets, kept the boys going through the hard times.

quite believe it – as you can tell from the backstage YouTube video.

On the way back to the dressing room they bounced along the corridor. RM explained that he practised his speech that afternoon, praying that they might win. He had worked it all out and had been planning to mention their families, their dance teachers and Big Hit staff. However, on reaching the microphone, he was so overcome that he just bleated out 'Bang Si-hyuk PD-nim', the formal name of the Big Hit boss. Luckily, Suga whispered to him that they should also thank their parents.

If this was a good end to 2013, picking up the Rising Star prize at the Golden Disc Awards on 1 January was the perfect start to 2014. Winning the debut award at the oldest of the Korean Music Awards ceremonies put BTS in good company – successful groups such as Super Junior, SHINee and EXO had all been previous winners.

At the end of January, they picked up another rookie gong. Following

BANGTAN BOMB

N.O TROT VERSION BY JUNGKOOK AND OPERA VERSION BY BTS

This is *O!RUL8,2?*-era gold. Jungkook is backstage, passing the time by singing a trot (a traditional Korean-style ballad) version of the 'N.O' refrain. Urged on by Suga, the others try different styles, topped by the most stunning operatic high note from J-Hope. You'll laugh – and be impressed!

in EXO's footsteps again, they won Best New Artist at the Seoul Music Awards. It was perfect timing, because the countdown to the final part of the trilogy – *Skool Luv Affair* – had begun. The concept teaser photos continued with the schoolboy theme, with the guys posing in school uniform and heavy eye make-up. The comeback trailer featured RM delivering a heavy rap over a fantastic animated sequence of old-school hip-hop iconography, including guys with beatboxes for heads.

On 11 February came the live TV showcase for the mini-album, with the boys performing the track 'Jump' – with exuberant choreography to match, including a mid-air hand chair for Suga to sit and rap in – and, highlighted by a flying J-Hope, the lead track, 'Boy in Luv'.

The new concept positioned the group as the school bad boys, tough and wild but with tender hearts as the EP took the themes of young love and romance. The look was school uniform – black jackets (rebel Jimin ditching his for a leather one), white shirts and black trousers – worn with attitude. Jimin's coconut hair had gone and was now gelled up and messy, V went for an interesting bright orange, while RM sported a slicked-back silver quiff.

The video for 'Boy in Luv' followed the concept. They're a school gang. Jungkook is the only one doing any schoolwork. The others are hiding away or messing about until the sight of a pretty girl walking down the corridor brings them together. To get her in front of Jungkook, they rap in her face, grab her wrist and pull her along – it doesn't look great, but their attitudes to women will soon change for the better.

On YouTube, they demonstrated 'Boy in Luv' for a 'Let's Dance' video. This series allows artists and groups to teach fans their dance moves. Taking us through their macho-romantic number, V and Jungkook demonstrated the 'King Kong', all swinging arms and beating chests; Jin and Jimin showed us the 'Shaving Dance', a preening, posing routine ending on a 'hey!'; and finally the rap line showed us their as-yet-unnamed, tough-guy, grab-your-pants sequence. Just copy that rough but vulnerable look and you too can dance like BTS!

> Copy that rough but vulnerable look and you too can dance like BTS!

The CD package came in a smooth, green case with metallic pink lettering. As with the previous CD boxes, it was accompanied by an extensive photobook and collectible extras: a sticker pack of animated hip-hop monster Bangtans, a random group photo card and a random band member card backed with some 'scribbled' personal details, including their date of birth, blood group, favourite things and a signature.

Without abandoning their hip-hop style, in *Skool Luv Affair* the tracks have a stronger vocal element than previous albums. RM, Suga and J-Hope all contribute to the lyrics and Suga was involved in writing and arranging nearly all the songs.

Remember the 'Outro: Luv in Skool' backing track? Here it is again as 'Intro: Skool Luv Affair', which takes hold as the boys give us their personal take on romance. 'Boy in Luv' begins with classic BTS hip-hop, but after a minute or so something new happens and the mood completely changes. The usual electronic dance sound is suddenly replaced with electric guitars and drums – have BTS become a rock band? Well, no, but just nine months after debut they are showing they are willing and able to play around with their sound.

Previous BTS love songs fixated on past romances and the bittersweet memories of recently finished relationships, but this track is different. Here the guys are tough but humbled by a girl who seems tantalizingly unattainable. They are insecure, frustrated, confrontational, sensitive and vulnerable – all in one song! It's another great teen anthem in which RM gets angry for being made to look stupid in front of the girl, J-Hope tries to stay tough, while in a classic line Jungkook asks his dad for advice. How did he ask his mum out? Did he write a letter? So sweet!

'Skit: Soulmate', a classic skit showing a discussion about what they are going to do for a skit – with rare appearances from special guests Supreme Boi and Bang PD – is up next, followed by 'Where Did You Come From?' with its super-bouncy and fun synth sound. The song is another *Satoori* dialect-themed song as the boys compete with their chat-up lines.

'Just One Day' (which they promote in April as the second single from the album) is a smooth, lush track with a mid-tempo R&B-infused sound. Its dreamy lyrics describe a perfect twenty-four hours with their girl, although Suga, ever the realist, reminds us that with

BANGTAN BOMB

RINGA LINGA (BY TAEYANG OF BIGBANG) DANCE PARTY

The bombs are full of BTS boys singing and dancing to other artists' hits and this is a really funny early example. Jimin (just look at the hair!) seems to have the moves figured out pretty well, but J-Hope looks to be just arm-throwing and V doesn't get past the first few seconds. Still, they're having such a good time, so who's complaining?

BANGTAN BOMB

BOYS' CONFESSION THEIR OWN WAY

Watch this companion piece to 'Where Did You Come From?' in which each of them try out their 'love confession' chat-up lines to camera. Who's your winner? Would your heart be captured by Jin's intensity, Jimin's, er, cheesy acting, V's toughness, Jungkook's smile or J-Hope's pure madness? (Let's be honest – Suga just isn't trying hard enough!)

their busy schedule it is just a dream. When the video emerged – on a minimalist set with the boys in white cardigans, sitting on chairs and showing a new sweet and sensitive side – it undoubtedly recruited another legion of fans to ARMY.

But if you thought BTS had forsaken rap for good, think again. The next three tracks see them return to their hip-hop roots. 'Tomorrow' continues the 'follow your dream' theme as RM spits out some machine-gun fast rap, while 'Cypher Pt. 2: Triptych' lets the rap line loose, with Suga, intense and sincere, perhaps at his best. Then there's 'Spine Breaker', which has become a firm fan favourite. It is a classic, socially aware BTS song, which, over V's superb, deep melody, points to the cost – both financially and to society – of kids slavishly following expensive fashions.

The album draws to a conclusion with the excellent 'Jump', an up-tempo celebration of years of hard work that really comes into its own on stage. Finally, the vocal line is given a pure, two-minute ballad to sing out the album and for some, this is when Jin, effortlessly hitting those high notes, really shines for the first time.

If there were any doubts about the course BTS were taking, *Skool Luv Affair* and 'Boy in Luv' had firmly dispelled them. The future was suddenly looking pretty rosy as the album went to number one in the Korean chart and number three in the Billboard World Albums Chart. 'Boy in Luv' also hit number five on the Billboard World Chart, which ranks the best-performing international digital singles in the US. As summer approached, with prime-time TV appearances and a trip to Japan coming up, there was little doubt – BTS really were the rookie kings.

RM

FACT FILE

Name: Kim Namjoon
Nicknames: RM, Rap Monster, God of
Destruction, Dance Prodigy, Namjoonie
Date of Birth: 12 September 1994
Birthplace: Ilsan, South Korea
Height: 1.81 metres (5'11")
Education: Apgujeong High School, Global
Cyber University
Chinese zodiac: Dog
Star sign: Virgo

FOUR

KIM NAMJOON/RM:
THE MONSTER WITHIN

He's no monster, he's Kim Namjoon: the quietly spoken leader of BTS. The rapper is the tallest and arguably the most stylish of the group, and has proved to be both sensitive and deep-thinking. So when, in September 2017, he announced he was changing his name to RM, it seemed a natural transition – the teenage rapper who had taken the macho name Rap Monster as a Big Hit trainee has since shown himself to be a super-intelligent and accomplished musician – more poet than monster.

Kim Namjoon grew up in Ilsan, an affluent satellite city of Seoul in South Korea, with his mum, dad and younger sister. A happy boy, his smiling childhood photos reveal those same dimples that ARMY swoon over twenty years later. School was never a problem for a young Namjoon. Despite admitting to acting up as the class clown, he studied hard and consistently earned good grades. As far as his parents were concerned, a top university and a good job beckoned. Looking at Namjoon's middle-school graduation photo, with his shapeless pudding haircut and unfashionable glasses, you'd be forgiven for having him down as a future government official.

At home, his mother encouraged Namjoon to learn English. Together they would watch CNN and BBC News programmes, and when he was twelve he went to New Zealand to study for four months. As he revealed on the US *Ellen DeGeneres Show* in 2017, 'My English teacher was the sitcom *Friends*. Back in the day, when I was like fifteen, fourteen, it was quite like a syndrome for all the Korean parents to make their kids watch *Friends*.' He explained that his mother bought him all ten seasons on DVD: 'So firstly, I watched them with the Korean subtitles, and then next time I watched with the English subtitles, and then I just removed it.'

Around this time he discovered another English-language tutor: rap music, especially US artists like Nas and Eminem. He began to write his own rap lyrics on scraps of paper, hiding them between the pages of his schoolbooks so his parents didn't learn about his passion. He was occasionally found out, but no one really minded as long as he continued to receive stellar grades in his schoolwork. By now he was being encouraged to look way beyond his elementary school ambition of being a concierge (although he did eventually get to wear the uniform in the 'Dope' music video!).

He began to write his own rap lyrics on scraps of paper.

Namjoon was developing fast as a rapper, too. He took the stage name Runch Randa, from an avatar in the video game *Maple Story*, and would hang out in Hongdae, the trendy neighbourhood of Seoul, where the hip-hop scene (known as the underground) was flourishing. Along with some others, including Kidoh (formerly of Topp Dogg), rapper Iron and future BTS producer Supreme Boi, he put together a rap crew named DaeNamHyup (or DNH), and later hooked up with other rising stars, including Zico, now leader of Block B.

Soon he was turning heads. In 2010, the hip-hop artist and TV celebrity, Sleepy, attended an underground crew audition and spotted this young kid with a gift for rapping. He got the phone number of Runch Randa, called Big Hit Entertainment and told them they might like to take a look at this talented high-school freshman.

But his teachers and parents still had other plans for him. In his Korean language, maths, foreign language and social studies exams, Namjoon really excelled. A test gave him an IQ of 148, and he came close to being in the top 1 per cent of students in the whole country. Crunch time was getting nearer for Namjoon, but how could he convince his parents that a career in music was the right path?

He told the Koreaboo website that he put forward a carefully crafted argument. 'My grades were about five-thousandth place in the country,' he recalled telling his mother. 'If I were to keep going on the path I was, I would've been a successful man with a plain job. But, no matter how smart people told me I was, I was five-thousandth in the country. However, I was positive I'd be number one in the country when it came to rap.' He asked his mum whether she wanted her son to be first or five-thousandth. What mother could refuse her child such an opportunity?

'I was positive I'd be number one in the country when it came to rap.'

Namjoon passed his audition at Big Hit in 2010 and worked with the company as a solo rapper and then as they tried various combinations of rappers to create a hip-hop group called Bangtan Sonyeondan. Some left, frustrated with the process, while others quit when Big Hit decided to change the focus and develop an idol group.

And so began Namjoon's three long years as a trainee. These were tough, boring and repetitive days of hard work, which included dance, a new discipline for Namjoon. He hadn't signed on as a dancer, but that came as part of being an idol group, so he worked at it, picking up a new nickname, Dance Prodigy – an ironic reference to his struggles as a dancer – in the process. Even as recently as 2015 he said he still didn't like dancing, but he understood it was part of the deal.

It was as a trainee that he picked up the Rap Monster moniker. At the very end of one of his songs, he would yell out 'Rap Monster!', and company staff started calling him by that name for fun. It stuck and he took it as his stage name. It was one of many changes he would make as BTS approached debut. He was often criticized for selling out and abandoning the true underground rap path, and consequently had to defend himself for signing up as an idol and enjoying the opportunities it provided; he also sometimes found idol life difficult and wasn't always comfortable wearing smoky make-up, pulling cutsie *aegyo* poses and performing those highly choreographed dances.

Of course, there was one other major change that Namjoon had to deal with: he was named leader of BTS. This was a great honour, but it was also a position that came with a great deal of responsibility. In public appearances such as promotions, tours and comeback press conferences, awards acceptance speeches and TV interviews, he would have to take charge. He would have to be articulate and authoritative, but also make sure he included the rest of the group, giving them the opportunity to contribute and comment. Considering their astonishing future success in the USA, it was a far-sighted move by Big Hit to give leadership of the group to its best English speaker.

The leader also has to represent the group to the company and the company to the group. In a fascinating episode of the Korean TV series *Problematic Men*, RM and Suho from boy group EXO discuss group leadership. RM explains how he was made leader because he was the first member of BTS and his ideas contributed to the musical direction of the group, despite not being the eldest. Jin, Suga and J-Hope are all his seniors (an important distinction in Korean society), which, when he has to take charge, can sometimes create a little friction. The way he deals with his responsibilities doesn't go unnoticed by the others, though. In the *Wings* concept book, a grateful V points out how RM takes many of the problems on his own shoulders and works hard to create an atmosphere in which the members of BTS get along well.

> RM takes many of the problems on his own shoulders and works hard to create an atmosphere in which the members of BTS get along well.

Despite being leader, RM is close to all of the members of the group. His naturally reserved nature, and his work as a songwriter and producer, mean that in backstage videos he is often seen quietly sitting in the background, preparing for the performance, but in the reality series *Gayo* or *Run BTS!* we can see how he takes part in playing games, silly dancing and messing around with the others.

Of all the band members, he has known Suga the longest, having befriended the boy from Daegu when he turned up in the dorm in 2011. These two are the serious musicians of the group and have a deep understanding of each other – RM has admitted that Suga is the one he turns to when he is worried. Then there are his other former roommates: Jungkook, who has a special 'big brother' relationship with RM (watch V-Live's 'One-Minute English' to see this in action as RM teaches the young *maknae* to say 'Pardon?'), and V, the member who seemed to miss him most when he had to return home early on the first *Bon Voyage* trip (one of BTS's unsupervised trips abroad).

Namjoon and Jin's bond is over their position as worst dancer! Jin told the TV show *Please Take Care of My Refrigerator* that in their choreography practice, the other five members learn from the dance instructor while he and RM are excluded and end up learning the moves in the corner.

In terms of pure personality, fellow 94-liner J-Hope (he and RM were both born in 1994) can always get RM laughing, particularly with his cheeky impressions of the leader. Indeed, RM has said J-Hope would be his ideal desert-island companion – because his constant talking would mean RM wouldn't need a radio!

RM has said J-Hope would be his ideal desert-island companion – because his constant talking would mean RM wouldn't need a radio!

J-Hope also features in one of RM's most memorable acting roles: as the mother to RM's hilarious BTS-loving, tantrum-throwing schoolgirl in the 2017 'House of Army' video. This clip would feature in any RM highlights roll, alongside his brilliant flailing-sleeve comic dance on *Weekly Idol*, in which he keeps a poker-straight face as bemused fellow members look on (except Suga, who can't bear to watch!), his tragic attempt at cutting an onion on the same programme and, of course, his inspired aeroplane seat utterance of 'Jimin, you got no jams'.

Over the formative years of BTS, as well as the rapper and BTS leader RM, fans have also got to know the real Kim Namjoon. His clumsiness is legendary and he apparently breaks almost everything he touches, causing the other boys to nickname him the God of Destruction. The video clip of him breaking his brand-new sunglasses became an instant meme, but over the years we've also heard of doors falling off in the dorm and out-takes show him effortlessly smashing video props. Jin once told *Haru Hana* magazine that his leader was 'the

Baby Dinosaur Dolly', saying 'RM shakes his tail and crushes things'. Similarly, RM has an ability to lose things so often that none of them seemed at all surprised when he lost his passport and had to cut short his *Bon Voyage* trip to Scandinavia.

Group members have also been quick to separate RM's stage persona from the Namjoon who shares their dorm. Suga said in an *Ize* magazine interview that, on the stage, Rap Mon wears sunglasses and gives out a powerful image, but really he likes cute things. Indeed, Namjoon has a dog called Rapmon, an adorable fluffy white American Eskimo Dog, which he got as a puppy back in 2013. Then there is his obsession with Ryan, the lovable lion character from the instant messaging app Kakao Friends. He has admitted to having at least thirteen stuffed Ryans in his dorm room, as well as a set of Ryan pyjamas, a Ryan eye mask and Ryan phone cases – and in 2016 the others even gave him a Ryan birthday cake.

BANGTAN BOMB

JIMIN: I GOT YES JAM

Two minutes of joyous wigging out as RM bonds with Jimin in an all-out dance frenzy. An ARMY favourite, this bomb features a lot of jumping around, plenty of air-guitar action and proof that Kim Namjoon is as capable as anyone of just flipping out. And remember, as the man himself once said, it's R-A-P Monster, not D-A-N-C-E Monster!

RM's outfits are another key aspect of his character. He posts regular pictures of himself using the hashtag #KimDaily on BTS's official Twitter account. His style is dominated by high-fashion streetwear, with an emphasis on black and white, but he's not afraid to mix in a colourful shirt or accessory. You'll usually find him wearing a cap or a beanie and classic Converse or Vans, but he puts together his own style, often with Japanese brands such as WTAPS and Neighborhood. RM can carry off most looks, even ones you might call quirky, as his unforgettable Minion dungarees outfit from 2015 surely proves!

It is, however, the reflective side of Namjoon that many ARMY most admire. You will often find the words 'sexy brain' in posts from fans whose favourite is RM. He is interested in new ideas, philosophy and politics, and is a committed reader. He likes the Japanese authors Haruki Murakami and Hitomi Kanehara, writers such as Kafka and Camus, and has particularly recommended British novelist Jojo Moyes's love story *Me Before You*.

> Namjoon is interested in new ideas, philosophy and politics, and is a committed reader.

For many fans, part of the appeal is that he agonizes over details and takes issues to heart. Hurt by criticism in BTS's early days, he has apologized publicly for issues of perceived racism, sexism and plagiarism. For later concepts he undertook his own research, such as reading Tony Porter's thought-provoking *Breaking Out of the Man Box: The Next Generation of Manhood* or consulting with feminist academics.

This image of RM as a deep thinker emerges in his *Wings* song 'Reflection', in which he describes how, if he has something on his mind, he takes time out by going to Ttukseom Island in Seoul to think it through. In an interview in January 2018, he revealed that in the past he always coped with anxiety by immersing himself in music, but he has now developed other 'escapes', such as shopping for clothes, collecting toy figures and connecting with the real world by taking a random bus journey to a new place.

In 2015, Rap Monster, as he then was, dropped a mixtape (a type of non-commercial album favoured by rappers) that played on this introspection. His announcement of the release of *RM* on Twitter ended with 'U do u, I do I', and its theme was the difficulty of discovering your individuality. The track 'Do You' debates whether to swim with or fight against the current, while 'Awakening' discloses his journey to being a proud idol rapper. *RM* would win a place in *Spin* magazine's list of the fifty best hip-hop albums of the year, and the mixtape proved that he could be both an idol star and a 'real' rapper.

That status was confirmed by subsequent collaborations with Wale and Fall Out Boy, but it is RM's increasing contributions to BTS recordings that mark his progress since the mixtape, with most of the songs on *Love Yourself: Her* and *Love Yourself: Tear* featuring significant songwriting and production input from RM. Since he first joined Big Hit, he admits he's had plenty of growing up to do. He's lost the tough-boy image, the toothbrush hairstyles and, eventually, the Rap Monster stage name, but in their place has appeared RM, a talented, grounded and thoughtful character – who is not a million miles away from a certain Kim Namjoon.

FIVE

AMERICAN HUSTLERS

Korean television variety shows are essential exposure for K-pop bands making their way in the world, and on 1 April 2014 BTS were excited to make their TV debut on the *Beatles Code* show. They performed their Bangtan greeting in slow motion, J-Hope showed his street-dancing skills and Jungkook performed press-ups while singer Park Ji-yoon sat on him. For first-timers, they came across very well.

Then, on 30 April 2014, to great anticipation, BTS featured on the big one, the show that's a must for everyone who is anyone in K-pop: the long-running and popular variety show *Weekly Idol* where stars are interviewed but also teased and set amusing tasks. Dressed down in ripped jeans, tees and long shirts, they looked more comfortable than ever. In a rapping test, Jin hilariously shows why he's in the vocal line, while V completely smashed it, and in the random dance section, where the boys had to remember their own dance moves, poor Jimin got it all wrong and the presenters described him as a 'lost sheep'. It was very funny! Finally, the Initial Profiles section, where guests showcase their special skills, became the Jungkook show. He danced move for move to half- and double-speed versions of 'Boy in Luv' and then danced brilliantly to Girl's Day's 'Something'. It's still a must-see for any

Kookie lover. For young and still shy boys, they had made a fine start.

Having established a following in South Korea, it was now time for Bangtan to spread their wings. In mid-April they spent a few days in China, where they were amazed to find so many ARMY at the airport. Word had spread far and fast, and *China Job*, a documentary about the trip, showed them attending the V Chart Awards, where they performed in black suits and red sneakers, and picked up another newcomer award.

> Having established a growing following in South Korea, it was now time for Bangtan to spread their wings.

In early summer, the focus turned to Japan. Under the name Bōdan Shōnendan (the Japanese form of Bangtan Sonyeondan), they were about to release a Japanese version of 'No More Dream', and on 31 May they flew out to Tokyo to meet and perform the song for 5,000 of their Japanese ARMY at the Dome City Hall (adding an afternoon performance due to high demand). It was the start of something big there, and they would soon be back.

Russia also got a look at the boys in June when the band travelled to the Bridge to Korea festival in Moscow. This event was designed to bring tourists to both countries, and they judged a K-pop dance competition and performed in front of the Kremlin to a crowd of over 10,000. Dressed in their grey cardigan outfits, they did a twenty-minute medley of hits followed by a joyous, out-of-tune, almost punk version of the traditional Korean folk song and unofficial anthem 'Arirang'.

A year had now gone by since BTS's debut – in fact it had flown by. On 13 June 2014, to mark the anniversary, they held their first *festa* (a Korean term for festival), releasing collections of photographs, dance videos and a fun-filled hour-long radio-style discussion show.

They also put out a new commemorative song, a rap-led track called 'So 4 More', which found them looking back at the ups and downs of the past year and wondering, in classic BTS fashion, whether the hardships were all worthwhile.

Back in the summer of 2012, Jungkook had travelled to Los Angeles to study at the famous Movement Lifestyle dance academy, but none of the others had set foot in the US. All Jungkook could tell them was that the air there was different, but now they were about to find out for themselves: they were on their way to LA.

When the boys landed in LA, it was time for a little sightseeing. They went to a baseball game, where they caught countryman

BANGTAN BOMB

LET'S SPEAK ENGLISH!

This is probably the most famous of all Bangtan bombs. The boys are on the plane flying into LA and J-Hope decides they need to practise their English. Of course, RM, as a fluent English speaker, chats away and J-Hope gives it a go with some adorable broken English, but the others aren't really playing. Expressing his disappointment, J-Hope tells RM that Jimin really isn't any fun, to which RM makes the iconic reply: 'Jimin, you got no jams!' In Korean, *jaemi* means fun, so RM is making up his own English slang. It is now an essential part of BTS history.

Hyun-jin Ryu pitching for the Dodgers, and they hit the beach and showed off their dance moves in Santa Monica. As it was getting dark, they pulled into a parking lot and waited in the van while their manager went off to run an errand until, all of a sudden, in burst three scary-looking men. BTS were being kidnapped!

Was this for real? Well, no, fortunately it was a prank, filmed for the opening of their reality series *American Hustle Life*. Were the boys in on the joke? Possibly, but Jungkook and J-Hope appeared genuinely terrified as, driven to what looked like a seedy part of town, the band members were hustled into a warehouse apartment and told to sleep. At 6 a.m., jet-lagged and dozy, they were woken by none other than US rap star Coolio and his team of rap mentors. They were about to get a crash course in American hip-hop life.

They were about to get a crash course in American hip-hop life.

Over the eight episodes of *American Hustle Life* the boys are set challenges, but this isn't light and frothy, it's hardcore, and Coolio and his crew take the hip-hop boot-camp idea seriously. Poor V discovers this pretty quickly as he tries to lighten the mood by jokingly saying, 'Let's go party. Turn up!' He is immediately punished with twenty-five push-ups. 'Quit playing with me,' barks Coolio. 'If it wasn't for hip-hop, I'd be dead or in jail.' To this day, some ARMY still resent the way the veteran rap star talks to V – 'Let me know when he leaves,' says Coolio coldly at one point – and Suga and Jin fall out with their mentor Dante so badly that after episode two he isn't seen again.

As they take on tasks including presenting a cooking segment, calling at strangers' homes to perform for them and finding girls to invite to dance in their music video, the boys sometimes appear confused, awkward and vulnerable. However, they are wonderful in their determination to please their mentors, the way they help each other along, and, of course, their charm and talent shines through. In the dance battle, J-Hope shows that despite the complexity of BTS choreography, he still has moves to spare; when he's not charming *noonas* (older ladies) in the market, V's vocals completely bowl over singing teacher Iris; and Suga comes into his own writing brilliant new lyrics for Warren G's 'Regulate'.

Seeing each of the group in trying situations does give us a great picture of BTS at this stage of their career. They clearly learn some lessons, especially in dealing with people. They have to meet ordinary folk and work mundane jobs, sometimes for mean bosses (Jimin and RM cleaning the bathroom is comedy gold), and they even have to talk to girls. As mentor Tony told the MoonROK website, 'I know the Korean entertainment culture is very strict about relationships, so when we put them in front of girls, they were so shy. They didn't know what to do.'

> Seeing each of the group in trying situations does give us a great picture of BTS at this stage of their career.

The bond that the great Warren G, who turns up in a stretch limo to give them a tour of his Long Beach hometown, has with his fans clearly resonated with the boys, especially as it was now time for BTS to meet their American public. Early in the morning on 13 July 2014 they announced on Twitter that the following day they would be playing a 'show and prove' concert at the Troubadour rock club in West Hollywood in which they would show what they had learned in the US. Entry was free – but was limited to just 200 people. No wonder the queue went right round the block. True to their word, they performed their singles along with covers of 'Regulate' and, with proud singing coach Iris (the real-life inspiration for *Sister Act 2*) watching from the balcony, the gospel classic 'Oh Happy Day!'.

In North America there is a large US-Korean population and K-pop is firmly established there, while K-pop groups are regularly promoted in the Far East. These music industries provide a new group like BTS with a platform to build on. Europe, with its very limited exposure to K-pop, however, would provide a different set of challenges. Summer 2014 saw BTS making an attempt to crack Europe as they took their first trip there, with showcases and fan meets in Berlin and Stockholm. These shows were mobbed by small but fanatical crowds as the boys performed their *Skool* trilogy hits. Their online presence and successes in other parts of the world were clearly getting BTS recognition in all corners of the globe.

In August, they made their first visit to Brazil, a country where they would find some of their most committed followers. In a short space of time they learned a lot about the country, including not to get off the plane in shorts and T-shirts when it's winter! In the Via Marquês club, BTS introduced themselves in Portuguese and talked about their impressions of Brazil, Jin saying he could already feel it was 'the country of passions' and Suga remarking that he had heard Brazil has many hot girls and, looking at the audience, he could now confirm that fact for himself! Wherever they went, they were making friends and gaining fans for life.

LA wasn't quite finished with BTS for the summer. In another big break for the now-no-longer rookie group, they were booked to play at KCON 2014. Over the course of a weekend, KCON, which began in 2012, celebrates K-drama, K-pop, Korean fashion and Korean food. This was their chance to show America what they were really about – and they didn't disappoint. Their red-carpet appearance delighted everyone; the BTS hi-touch and sign session was the hottest ticket around; and fans waited hours in the intense heat to catch their special appearance on *Danny From L.A.*, a US K-pop TV show.

However, the evening concerts were the highlight and, as anyone attending KCON 2014 soon realized from the fans' T-shirts and banners, BTS might not have been the headliners (that was G-Dragon and Girls' Generation), but they were a major attraction. The crowd, many of whom already seemed to know the chants and the members' names, were loud and wildly enthusiastic. The show went down a storm with those unfamiliar with BTS, too, and an *LA Times* correspondent commented, 'The group made the strongest impression of all the US debuting acts. This won't be the last time they play to thrilled crowds in the States.'

It had been a busy summer of filming and touring, but that was

BANGTAN BOMB

(EYES, NOSE, LIPS) OF BTS

Taeyang's 'Eyes, Nose, Lips', an emotional R&B-style track about remembering an ex, was the song of the summer 2014 in Korea and beyond. In this priceless clip, the Bangtan Boys give us their own unique take on the song. Eavesdrop as they lip-sync, over-act, fool around and even sing along. They all have a go, even RM, who initially turns his back to escape the camera, and V, who overcomes his shyness in the end.

just the half of it. Wherever they went – Seoul, America, Europe, Brazil – they were writing and recording new material, and dancing to the point of exhaustion. Watch the music video for '24/7 = Heaven' to see them hard at work in nondescript practice rooms around the world. And, when in LA, as well as the stress of *American Hustle Life*, they were laying down tracks in a studio set up in the garage of Bang Si-hyuk's apartment. The result was their first full-length album.

The comeback trailer for *Dark & Wild* was released on 5 August 2014. It featured RM's 'What Am I To You', a feverish track about a frustrated and insecure romance. A few days later, as a pre-release, they started streaming 'Let Me Know', another stirring, desperate song, on their website. Suga, who co-wrote the track, had promised fans they would love the song for its trance-like melody, and he wasn't wrong. ARMY held their breath for the full release.

The *Dark & Wild* concept photos revealed a more mature look that matched the more grown-up tone of the new songs. The bad-boy image was still there and they were back in black, but with stylish leather jackets and trousers with white T-shirts. The gold chains and rings had returned, but again in a more subdued way, and the boys looked serious and thoughtful as they stared into or away from the camera, despite the fact that Suga and J-Hope's hair was bright red and Jin's a subtle purple (which proved pretty popular with his fans).

The music video for 'Danger', the album's lead track, was released on 19 August 2014. The boys wore denim jackets and ripped jeans, but the overall feel was still dark. There is no real storyline this time, just brooding imagery. The settings are depressing – a disused subway and a derelict warehouse, partially flooded and littered with burning shopping carts – and the members play characters hurt by love. They try to distract themselves – RM writes, Suga plays basketball, J-Hope

BANGTAN BOMB

RUNWAY IN THE NIGHT

What to do when you're all dressed up with nowhere to go? How about turning a corridor into your own model runway? That's the BTS answer as they wait around in their 'Danger' finery. From then on it's just a matter of who can goof around most. J-Hope's always a good bet, Jin certainly has the moves and V is, well, V.

dances – but it's no use. As their frustrations spill over, Jimin lays into a punchbag, Jin plays with fire and Jungkook smashes up a piano, while RM takes a tattoo needle to his arm and V sets about cutting his own hair.

In the YouTube clip on the making of the music video you can see that they actually had a lot of fun portraying the darker side of youth. However, Jimin admits he's embarrassed about the boxing, RM notes that their trainers haven't dried from dancing in the water and V announces that, despite wearing a wig, he somehow managed to cut his real hair! Jungkook also reveals later that he ripped open his index finger destroying the piano, so couldn't use the fingerprint recognition system to get into the dorm and for several weeks had to wait for someone else to let him in.

The most impressive aspect of the video has to be the choreography. It has the usual hip-hop character, but it's smoothed out and the b-boy moves have been incorporated to create a distinct BTS style. As ever, they stay perfectly in sync, but watch as they introduce the 'high blood pressure' part of the dance with an attention-grabbing neck-rub and shrug of the shoulder, then transform the macho arm fold or crouch into something more emotional and expressive.

This may be where BTS dance came of age.

The CD was presented in a glossy black card case with random scratch marks and an official-looking warning in English about the effects of love. The package contained a highly collectible random individual photo card and group photo card, and a photobook with lyrics (in a bewitching handwritten style with doodles and underlinings), as well as a couple of postcards, one of the Hip-Hop Monster BTS characters and the other of characters from a forthcoming BTS web comic.

> This may be where BTS dance came of age.

In the album showcase, Suga stated that the previous single-album and mini-albums had been preparation for this, their first full album, and it should be listened to from beginning to end with the interlude bridging the change in tone from frustration to release. This was BTS growing up, no longer talking about school but focusing on the emotional stresses of youth.

> This was BTS growing up.

So after RM's opening rap, 'What Am I To You', 'Danger', the lead track on *Dark & Wild*, zeroes straight in on the emotional damage caused by unrequited love. The group has developed lyrically and progressed from 'please go out with me' songs to songs about love that can really hurt when it goes wrong, and the music has matured, too. The vocal line has more room to explore their harmonies, the backing brings in a guitar sound that persists above the percussion, and the rap seems relaxed and less stylized.

Despite being poppy and infectious, in 'War of Hormone' BTS court controversy again with their honesty about the effects of hormones on young men. They admit they are girl crazy and, although they did receive some bad press for their attitude to women and tarnishing the squeaky-clean image of K-pop, this is clearly a hymn to girls and their tongues are firmly in their cheeks (J-Hope even has a line about popping a pimple!).

In 'Hip Hop Lover' we discover what BTS had learned from their summer school as, with a much more American feel than before, they name-drop their rap heroes and take us through their hip-hop education. Suga's pre-released 'Let Me Know' comes next, followed by 'Rain', an often underrated, melancholic, jazz-infused number with a fabulous cameo from J-Hope. The dark half of the album then closes with 'Cypher Pt. 3: Killer' featuring Supreme Boi, another circle-room rap session and, again, this seems more polished and less derivative than previous cyphers.

After a brief 1970s disco-inspired interlude that never quite takes off, we enter the wild side. They are a group building their fan base through social media, yet they are bold enough to ask, 'Would You Turn Off Your Cellphone?' Do they look like your parents? No, but you can't deny the message: we're missing out on a personal connection if we live our lives through our phones.

'Blanket Kick' is a song of frustrated embarrassment; a sweet confession of kicking at the bed sheets as you remember how weirdly you acted in order to impress or how you missed a once-in-a-lifetime opportunity. Now relax. It's '24/7 = Heaven' and they are back in love again. To the poppiest of upbeat grooves, a fine line distribution enables every one of them to feel the romance.

Putting out a full album meant BTS could push their boundaries a little and the next track, 'Look Here', sounds exactly like a group who had spent their summer in the US, hanging out in LA listening to Pharrell Williams's 'Come Get It Bae'. It's a light and breezy, percussion-based track and, of course, BTS sound as though they've been playing American-style pop all their lives.

After the penultimate track, '2nd Grade', a fun freak-out with a magnificent 'bang it, bang it' refrain, the record closes with 'Outro: Does That Make Sense?'. Here the album comes full circle to take up the theme of love grown cold once again. As on previous albums, the vocal line is called upon to finish, and right from Jungkook's delicious 'listen', they are smooth as silk and totally in the groove.

On the TV music-show promotions, the group's performances got more air time and ARMY stepped up a gear with fan chants clearly audible to viewers. Nevertheless, the show victory that BTS craved still eluded them. In a typical response, they vowed to work even harder.

JIN

FACT FILE

Name: Kim Seokjin

Nicknames: Jin, Worldwide Handsome, Visual King, Third One From The Left, Car Door Guy, Flying Kiss Guy, Granny

Date of birth: 4 December 1992

Birthplace: Angyang, Gyeonggi Province, South Korea

Height: 1.79 metres (5'10")

Education: Bosung High School, Konkuk University, Global Cyber University

Chinese zodiac: Monkey

Star sign: Sagittarius

SIX

KIM SEOKJIN/JIN: WORLDWIDE HANDSOME

fter the group's magenta carpet appearance at the Billboard Music Awards (BBMAs) in 2017, the hashtag #ThirdOneFromTheLeft suddenly went viral. It wasn't even the first time Jin had sent social media spinning. After his appearance at the 2015 Melon Awards, it was #CarDoorGuy that set Twitter ablaze. So what was he doing to attract such attention? Absolutely nothing. Unless you count being devastatingly good-looking. 'I think I'm worldwide handsome,' Jin explained. It wasn't exactly a modest statement, but nobody was arguing.

It was his looks – broad shoulders and a small face with what plastic surgeons call a 'golden ratio' of symmetrical features – that originally brought him to BTS. SM, one of the Big Three entertainment companies, had selected him in a streetcast, but he ignored their invite to audition (some say he actually ran away from the scouts), believing it was a prank. When Big Hit invited him along, he turned up, auditioned as an actor and found himself as the first non-rapper to join the group.

Kim Seokjin grew up in Gwacheon City, just south of Seoul. His family was tight-knit and he describes his childhood as idyllic. They would take trips to places such as Japan, Australia and Europe, and his father would teach him golf and take him to ski resorts, where Jin found he had an aptitude for snowboarding. He had a warm if competitive relationship with his brother, who was just two years older, and in fact he remains close to all his family, especially his mother. For Parents' Day in 2015 he recorded a touching cover of Ra.D's track 'Mom', adding a sweet dedication to her.

At the Beautiful Moments concert in Seoul his mother was in the audience and, as he welled up, he explained that his mum used to listen to her friends bragging about their sons without saying a word, so he really wanted to make his mum proud, and now, thanks to ARMY, he could. He is just as close to her today, with other members of the group remarking that he can stay on the phone to her for over an hour!

> He really wanted to make his mum proud, and now, thanks to ARMY, he could.

Jin's middle and high schools were both all-boy establishments and he admits to struggling to look girls in the eye, finally having to force himself to in order not to appear awkward in front of ARMY, but he did make plenty of friends, some of whom he is still in regular contact with despite his busy schedule. He enjoyed school, worked hard, played every possible sport and wanted to become a newspaper reporter.

That changed in 2009 when he watched the historical drama *The Great Queen Seondeok*, the most popular TV series in Korea. Like much of the nation, the young Seokjin was captivated, especially by the moving performance of actor Kim Nam-gil. It inspired the high-school student so much that he entered Konkuk University to major in acting at the Department of Film and Visual Arts. He had been studying for

Meet the baby-faced Bangtan Boys: performing on MBC Music's *Show Champion* in Seoul, South Korea, October 2013, just a few months after they debuted (above), and on the red carpet at the 3rd Gaon Chart K-pop Awards in Seoul, February 2014 (below).

RM

SUGA

JIN

J-HOPE

JIMIN

V

JUNGKOOK

Each one of the boys brings something different to the band; here they are at the Billboard Music Awards in Las Vegas, USA, in May 2018, looking handsome and sporting the matching dark hair that sent ARMY wild when they unveiled it for an LG advert.

Top: The boys rocking their street style on the red carpet at the Incheon Korean Music Wave photocall in Incheon, South Korea, September 2013.

Bottom: Showing how versatile their fashion choices already are in a dapper ensemble for another appearance on MBC Music's *Show Champion* in Ilsan, South Korea, March 2014.

Top: Back on the red carpet in maroon suits for the 5th Gaon Chart K-pop Awards, with Suga, RM and Jimin sporting some beautiful bright hair, Seoul, South Korea, February 2016.

Bottom: BTS burning up the stage in a live performance of 'Fire' at KCON in New Jersey, USA, June 2016.

'Worldwide Handsome' Jin went viral as the #ThirdOneFromTheLeft, but the rest of the boys were also looking good at the BBMAs in Las Vegas as they started to get some heat in the USA (above). Winning the award for 'Top Social Artist' was a huge deal for BTS, and they celebrated in style back home at a press conference in Seoul, South Korea, in May 2017 (below).

Top: The boys appearing on *Jimmy Kimmel Live!* where they treated fans to a set that included 'Go Go', 'Save Me', 'I Need U', 'Fire' and 'MIC Drop (Remix)', Los Angeles, USA, November 2017.

Bottom: Posing for the cameras backstage at the AMAs, Los Angeles, USA, November 2017.

BTS break America: on stage at the AMAs during a jaw-dropping
performance of 'DNA', Los Angeles, USA, November 2017.

just three months when he got the call from Big Hit in April 2011.

For a young guy who had set his heart on acting, trainee life must have been a massive shock. Luckily Seokjin's easy-going nature helped. When Bang Si-hyuk asked him to choose a one-syllable name as it is more intense, he simply shortened his own to Jin. He transformed himself from an aspiring actor into a trainee singer and dancer without fuss, saying he could always become an actor later. And he quickly got used to being the oldest in a group who could already dance, sing or rap. That was Jin, Mr No Worries.

But it wasn't easy. In the months before debut he found the dieting hard, and he struggled with performance skills, although he was always grateful to the other members of the group and the Big Hit staff who spent time helping him with his singing and his dance moves. Meanwhile, though, he had found his role in the dorm. It was soon evident that Jin was the one who would clean and tidy, put the groceries away and throw out rotten food. It was also clear that he loved cooking and creating meals to brighten up their somewhat tedious diet. No wonder that he soon picked up the nickname 'Granny' from his younger bandmates!

Perhaps at first Jin's shyness made him seem stand-offish to some of the members of BTS, but when he and Jungkook shared vocal lessons they quickly formed a bond. Jimin became his gym buddy and a love of animation brought him close to V. Suga never had any doubts: he shared a room with Jin and was adamant he never wanted to swap. Within the group, Jin was in an unfamiliar position: he was the eldest in this new 'family', having spent his life being the *maknae*, but again it didn't seem to bother him. He was quiet and serious with RM, J-Hope and Suga, and excitable and playful with the younger members, earning himself the label 'fake *maknae*'!

He still likes to cook for the others ... and looks after his pets, Odeng and Eomuk.

Within the dorm, Jin still takes on the 'parental' role. He rises two hours before his bandmates and makes sure they're awake and ready to start work on time (not always an easy task!). And, although they now have a cleaner, he still likes to cook for the others. Meanwhile, he continues to add to his collection of Super Mario figures (many given to him by fans) and looks after his pets, Odeng and Eomuk. He reportedly got these adorable sugar gliders, a type of small possum, after coming across them while searching for 'Suga' on the internet.

Like all the members of BTS, Jin has lots of friends in other idol groups. He is close to Ken from VIXX and they are both part of a 92-liner chat group along with B.A.P's Youngjae, BTOB's Eunkwang, B1A4's Sanduel and Baro, EXID's Hani, and Moonbyul from Mamamoo, who has said it's Jin and Sandeul who always make the chatroom interesting!

By March 2013, Jin's singing had progressed enough for him to join RM and Suga in recording 'Adult Child', one of the first pre-debut BTS tracks, on which he provides a simple but sweetly sung interlude. All was going pretty well for the seemingly unflappable Jin, but debut was to provide a shock for the senior member. He has told interviewers that the *M Countdown* show was the first time he had worn a microphone pack, and he had climbed on stage with it attached to his trousers. However, he had not accounted for the weight of the pack. During 'We Are Bulletproof Pt. 2', in the section where they jump down, his trousers slipped all the way down to his thighs. He quickly pulled them back up, but they fell off a second time. He laughs about it now, but at the time the poor boy was inconsolable.

Jin had few worries about his dancing before the BTS debut, but the criticism he received afterwards – some called him the 'black hole of dance' – hit home. He's worked hard at his dancing, but remains very modest about his talents on the dancefloor. In 2017 he told a TV show, 'I think I am really bad at dancing,' but added; 'however, Rap Monster really cannot dance!'

> 'I think I am really bad at dancing ... however, Rap Monster really cannot dance!'

An array of Seokjin talents have emerged since that debut day. No conversation with the Gwacheon boy seems to pass without an – often terrible – *ahjae* joke (literally an 'uncle joke', although in the West it's better known as a 'dad joke'). These are Korean puns or a joke made by mixing English with Korean, such as 'What does the dog say when it sees a wall?' The answer is 'Wol-wol', which is Korean for the sound a dog makes. No wonder the other members of BTS often look bemused or cringe with embarrassment! Perhaps of more use is Jin's dexterity with his toes. On various reality shows he has demonstrated his ability to open bags of sweets or take off his socks without using his hands. And how can we forget his signature 'Traffic police dance'? A hilarious marching, hand-waving move that he has even taught to the rest of the group.

Actually, reality shows have proved Jin to be both resourceful and fun. In January 2017, he appeared on the tough survival show *Law of the Jungle*, which sends celebrities to survive in remote locations around the world. Along with other K-pop stars and K-drama actors, he was packed off to rural Indonesia. Despite having to leave early to go on tour with BTS, Jin acquitted himself brilliantly. He proved popular with the other stars, made wooden paddles with a hand saw, caught fish using an ARMY bomb (light stick) as a fishing reel and cooked them for his jungle family, as well as winning water for his team with an acrobatic triple spin dive.

Jin's humour and energy would prove just as popular in other shows such as *Hello Counsellor* and *Please Take Care of My Refrigerator*, where he admitted the dorm fridge was mostly filled with cosmetics and that members would take food out to make room for them, and *Let's Eat Dinner Together*, where he entertained the crew with his *ahjae* humour and successfully found a Gangnam family willing to share their evening meal with him.

Ah, food! Jin loves his food. He loves cooking, eating and talking about food. His interest first surfaced on early Bangtan blogs when he would post 'Jin's Recipes' just to show how dull their debut diet food could be. This progressed to 'Jin's Cooking Diary', where he would detail more interesting meals, and eventually his V-Live series, *Eat Jin*. His version of *mukbang*, the popular videos where a host commentates as he or she eats, are a lot of fun, especially the episode where he attempts to consume an entire *jjajangmyeon* (a noodle and sauce dish favoured by Korean children) in one minute. One fan even decided to get a professional opinion on Jin's culinary skills. In 2017 she tweeted a photo of his noodles and fried egg to Gordon Ramsay, asking the British celebrity chef if Jin had any chance of winning his *Hell's Kitchen* series. The notoriously ill-tempered cook replied, 'Overcooked eggs with worms! No thanks.' Oh well, at least he didn't curse!

Jin's love for ARMY is also something else. He never fails to thank them for their support and has developed his own unique bond with them. It was Japanese ARMY who first called him 'Flying Kiss Guy' as they noticed his habit of blowing kisses off his hands to fans. He really has developed this into an art form, sending the most elegant and stylish kisses direct to every watching ARMY's heart.

For Jin really is the King of Hearts. It started with him putting out finger hearts to fans and drawing a heart on his hand next to the word 'ARMY', but it soon became his special contribution to the live show. In Hong Kong he reached into his shirt and produced a heart-shaped clothes hanger, in Anaheim he revealed a white heart taped over his heart, in Sydney he flicked back his sleeves to show his heart-shaped felt bracelets. He would produce giant fold-out hearts, a long paper concertina of hearts or suddenly turn around to display his heart-adorned glasses. The other members enjoy these surprises as much as the fans, especially Jungkook, who on tour in Osaka, Japan, searched Jin in vain for a heart, only to collapse in shocked laughter when the eldest member produced one from the microphone.

Though some ARMY worry on Jin's behalf that he doesn't get enough singing lines or screen time, Jin himself seems to have a zen-like contentedness about his place in BTS. The *Wings* album included the first song where he had contributed to the writing and he was

BANGTAN BOMB

BTS WITH SPECIAL MC JIN @2017 KBS

In December 2017, Jin was selected as one of the MCs for the KBS Gayo Festival, a televised seasonal pop extravaganza featuring top Idol acts. Feast your eyes on Mr Worldwide Handsome as he prepares – very seriously – for his role and see the rest of the group support him as they watch him on their dressing-room TV.

understandably proud of 'Awake', which he wrote with Pdogg. He says he worked hard on the writing and was very insistent his chorus was used. He was even reduced to tears when ARMY sang along to the song with him during a live performance. However, he doesn't expect to instantly become a major BTS songwriter. He says if his songs are included, great, but if they're not he'll keep working hard and new opportunities will arise. That's Jin: serenely taking everything in his stride. Perhaps it's easy to keep everything in perspective when you are Worldwide Handsome.

SEVEN

RED BULLETS

The city is in meltdown. An alien race of giant monsters is attacking Earth and we are defenceless. Our only hope is a tight-knit team of superheroes. With their special powers, they might just be able to fight off the mutant invaders. Fearless, self-sacrificing and incredibly handsome, they also look strangely familiar. Could this be BTS to the rescue?

We On: Be the Shield was an official Big Hit-promoted webtoon. It's a manga-style online comic telling a story of a team of superheroes determined to save the world. Think Marvel's *Avengers*, except this team has genius scientist RM; deadly accurate archer Jin; Suga, a warrior whose limbs become swords; J-Hope, the winged observer; Jimin, who can utilize the power of the natural world; Jungkook, whose body becomes armour to protect the team; and V, the summoner of darkness, shadows and deadly black holes.

It has so much more detail than this and is a great read for those who like their sci-fi fantasy mixed in with their favourite K-pop group. Uploaded in September 2014, it was more evidence that BTS were making themselves known. *Dark & Wild* had recently reached number two in Korea and number three in the Billboard World Albums Chart, 'Danger' had climbed to number seven on the Billboard World Digital

Songs Chart and in October they were to play in front of 5,000 fans in Seoul. They explained that BTS wanted to represent the energy of youth that will destroy obstacles and prejudice in the world, so the event was to be called 'The Red Bullet'. It was their first ever solo full-length concert.

The two AX Hall concerts sold out in five minutes, so an extra night was added. Headlining their own show was a big deal for BTS. 'Until now,' they told the press, 'we have stuck to the hip-hop genre and promoted concepts that differentiated us from other idol groups, so we are preparing a very unique concert.' And, sure enough, it was pretty special.

On each night, from 17 October through to 19 October 2014, they played an introductory video set in a classroom, followed by 150 minutes of Bangtan magic. They sang, danced and joked their way through a set of twenty-four songs, including, of course, hits such as 'Boy in Luv', 'Danger' and 'Just One Day', but also other favourites like 'Let Me Know', 'If I Ruled the World' and 'Blanket Kick', with its own bed and sofa on stage for extra *aegyo* and cuteness. The rappers, with a guest appearance from Supreme Boi, came together for 'Cypher Pt. 3: Killer', while the vocal line performed 'Outro' with a new second verse by Jin. As fans held up banners saying, in Korean, 'Let's walk on the same road together for life', they encored with a high-energy blast of 'Jump' and 'Rise of Bangtan', before finishing with the *Satoori* dialect rap, 'Paldogangsan'.

The audiences
were ecstatic
and sang along
with every
word.

The audiences were ecstatic and sang along with every word. Reflecting on the experience in their vlogs, the boys seemed shocked and slightly overwhelmed by the experience. They all admitted it was amazing, but felt it had passed like a dream. RM told the *Starcast* news channel, 'Our choreography is so extreme that it was a little bit scary, worrying whether we can really do it, but after the concert I felt much better, just like I had completed a bungee jump.' V, on the hand, picked 'War of Hormone' as the most memorable moment, saying, 'With other songs, it was full of tension, but when we sing this song, everyone was full of joy.'

Shortly after the concerts, on 23 October, BTS released 'War of Hormone' as a single, accompanied by a music video, which was the most fun they had had on screen to date. An impressive one-shot take in black and white, with some red splash added later for Jimin's trousers and the stripes on Jungkook's jumper, it has energy, laughs and the cheekiest choreography.

BANGTAN BOMB

'WAR OF HORMONE' IN HALLOWEEN

When you tire of watching the video for 'War of Hormone' (which, judging by some ARMY reaction, might take a while!) have a look at this special Bangtan bomb. In a rehearsal room festooned with spiders' webs, a costumed-up BTS perform the choreography – in character. RM is a vampire, Suga is knife-wielding Chucky, Jimin has dressed as Charlie Chaplin, Jin as Captain Jack Sparrow, V plays the Joker, J-Hope is prisoner Papillon and a whip-slinging Jungkook is anime character King of Terrors. Frightening? Not really. Fun? Totally!

The BTS Live Trilogy Episode II: The Red Bullet (to give it its full name) in Japan meant another first – a full concert in a different language. They had, however, cultivated a following in Japan, appearing on variety and music shows, and releasing Japanese-language singles of 'No More Dream', 'Boy in Luv' and 'Danger', all of which had made the Japanese top ten, so they were certainly among friends. Taking into consideration the traditionally reserved response of Japanese audiences, the shows in Kobe on 13 and 14 November and the 16 November performance in Tokyo were enthusiastically received – indeed, the fans knew all the words and sang along.

The boys returned to Seoul in time not only for Jin's birthday, which was coming up on 4 December, but also for the Mnet Asian Music Awards, which are arguably the most prestigious ceremony in the South Korean entertainment industry calendar. As the group were in their second year, it was thought to be unlikely that they would pick up a trophy, but BTS had been asked to perform. This alone was an achievement. J-Hope later told *Starcast*, 'To me, the stage at MAMA is the most memorable [event of the year]. When I performed at MAMA, I felt I had grown up ... I was so happy and excited.'

BTS performed 'Boy in Luv' during the show and came back for a display which set Twitter and the forums on fire. This was a section billed as 'The Fight of the Century', which pitted BTS against Block B, a similarly successful seven-boy, hip-hop-style group. The face-off took the form of a dance battle, a rap duel, a group performance and a joint performance – and the Bangtan Boys did ARMY proud. RM, in a white suit and pink shirt, went face to face with Block B's Zico, BTS put their all into 'Danger' and the two groups combined brilliantly for the Black Eyed Peas' 'Let's Get It Started'.

But it was the dance-off that really got fans talking. First, J-Hope, who took to the stage like a man possessed, pulled some breathtaking moves, once again proving that few could match him on the dancefloor. Then Jimin spun on to the stage and ripped off his hoody and T-shirt. The move looked slightly inelegant, and he later lamented that it was ten times cooler at rehearsal, but as he continued dancing without his shirt there were few complaints from those watching! Who won the battle? In a poll conducted over the next two weeks, BTS took 90.1 per cent of the votes. It was a great victory for both BTS and ARMY – a combination that would be mobilized again and again …

Before the end of the year and the TV music show Christmas specials, the Bangtan Boys had time to fly out and perform three more concerts in what had been named the Red Bullet tour. In Manila

BANGTAN BOMB

SOMEONE LIKE YOU (SUNG & PRODUCED BY V)

As the very end of the year approaches, so does V's birthday. In 2014, he decided to give a present back to ARMY in the form of his first cover song. On Twitter he asked fans what he should pick and someone suggested Adele's 'Someone Like You'. This, he said, has the kind of emotional vocals that appeal to him so that's what he went for. And, what's more, he planned and directed the video himself, shooting it in the back alley by the dorm in just sixteen minutes.

(7 December), Singapore (13 December) and Bangkok (20 December), BTS, with RM now sporting flaming red hair, gave every bit as good a performance as they had at their first concert in Seoul, while, for the first time outside Seoul, ARMY responded with surprise banners, fan chants and synchronized light-stick waving.

It was their second Christmas since debuting. Despite many in Korea doubting BTS's ability to win over new fans, they continued to prove these people wrong as their profile continued to grow. This year they appeared for the first time on the prestigious K-pop Christmas specials, *M Countdown Christmas Special* and the *Music Core End of the Year Special*. What's more, they were also invited to appear at *Seoul Countdown*, a New Year celebration outside the Lotte World Tower, Korea's tallest skyscraper. This was quite an honour, but look for Jungkook in the video of their performance on YouTube and you'll be disappointed – the Golden *Maknae* was still a minor and forbidden by law to work at such a late hour!

For those who like seeing the Bangtan Boys scrubbed up and smart, take a look at the range of outfits on display during the January 2015 awards season. They collected their *bonsan*g prize at the Seoul Music Awards in their school uniforms accessorized with waistcoats or cricket jumpers. To collect their World Rookie Award at the Gaon Chart K-Pop Awards they wore identical slimline, two-button grey jackets with black collars, black ties, black trousers and white shirts, while at the Golden Disc Awards they accepted their *bonsang* for *Dark & Wild* in more casual grey-brown jackets, green ties, white trousers and an assortment of shirts.

The fact that they were picking up *bonsangs* is a guide to where they ranked at this point in the K-pop standings. These are given for artists' achievements in the past year and it is not unusual for as many as ten *bonsangs* to be awarded in one category. BTS's ultimate ambition, however, was to win the *daesang* – the grand prize. To even dream of reaching that level they would first need to secure a win on a music show, which was now the immediate goal.

By the time 2015 really got underway, BTS had established themselves as one of the twenty best acts in Korea. That was pretty good for a group that lacked the backing of one of the Big Three, were helping write their own material and were still predominantly producing hip-hop-based music. But could they take their profile and performance up a notch?

It was certainly possible. ARMY were getting stronger by the day and the fan café was close to celebrating 100,000 members. They were getting airtime both as a group and individually (January saw V co-presenting *Best of the Best* on MTV with Suejong from Lovelyz, and RM had a TV job on the cards, too), and were now looking to build their overseas following with tours to both Japan and the US. Yet there was perhaps a sense that it was now or never. If they didn't win a TV music show, produce a number-one album or win the coveted grand prize of a *daesang* this year, would they fall by the wayside like many K-pop contenders before them?

One route to success lay in nearby Japan. Only the US music industry made more money than the Japanese; fans there were enthusiastic and the biggest buyers of physical CDs in the world, and they had a growing appetite for K-pop. BTS had laid down the foundations for success by recording Japanese versions of their hits and had taken the Red Bullet show to Kobe and Tokyo, but now they were preparing for a major assault on Japan.

The Japanese rapper, KM-MARKIT, who has worked with some

> Would they fall by the wayside like many K-pop contenders before them?

of the biggest names in Japanese hip-hop, had helped translate and rework BTS's Korean lyrics, enabling them to release their debut Japanese-language album, *Wake Up*, at the end of 2014. It contained Japanese versions of all their most popular songs, as well as three new tracks: 'Pt. 2 – At That Place', an answer song to 'I Like It'; 'The Stars', featuring some vocals from Jin; and 'Wake Up', which blended a soft Japanese-style rap with the BTS sound.

With the album reaching number two in the Japanese charts, BTS set off for Japan, where between 10 and 19 February they played to a total of 25,000 people in six sold-out concerts in Tokyo, Osaka, Nagoya and Fukuoka. Their set featured a sweet and funny video of them learning Japanese and, one by one, falling for the teacher, but each coming unstuck with their language mistakes, and they played the songs from *Wake Up* with some added surprises, such as pre-debut track 'Adult Child' and a cover of Mariah Carey's 'Beautiful'. As ever, they left the country with their profile enhanced and fans screaming for them to come back soon.

When they returned to Seoul, it was time for RM to take the limelight. And boy, was he busy! While recording a new mystery celebrity identity TV series called *Problematic Men* on which he was one of the hosts, he also released a collaborative single, 'P.D.D', with none other than Warren G, the pioneering rapper the group had met on *American Hustle Life*, and, finally, he dropped his long-awaited mixtape, titled *RM*.

Those paying close attention might have asked 'if Red Bullet is Episode II, what happened to Episode I?' BTS answered this by announcing two concerts, on 28 and 29 March 2015, at the Olympic Hall in Seoul titled 'Live Trilogy Episode I: BTS Begins'. The show was a review of their career so far – from the birth of the group to the Red

Bullet – and an opportunity to give a heartfelt thank you to ARMY and to their parents, some of whom were there, watching them perform live for the first time.

The boys, in piped blazers over white 'BTS Begins' hoodies, performed over twenty of their songs to an adoring audience. These included pre-debut songs like the Drake cover 'Too Much', as well as all their singles, and even a couple of sneak previews from their next short album. Two YouTube clips related to this concert are particular fan favourites. The first is a Bangtan TV video of J-Hope's astonishing dance practice for the event and the other is the clip of their last song of the evening: a fantastic performance of 'Born Singer', their pre-debut version of J. Cole's 'Born Sinner'. Watch them – they're brilliant!

BANGTAN BOMB

IT'S TRICKY IS TITLE! BTS, HERE WE GO! (BY RUN-DMC)

They might be in their Donna Karan finest (RM clearly didn't get the memo!), but what is great about this bomb is they're still kids having fun. Run-DMC's classic is an old favourite of theirs and as it plays they put together some cheeky, cheesy and impressive moves. First Jimin realizes he's missing out, then RM decides he wants to join in too and, hey, what about Jin? Fun and funky, this could be one of the best Bangtan bombs ever!

SUGA

FACT FILE

Name: Min Yoongi
Nicknames: Suga, Genius, Agust D, Syub
Energy, Motionless Min, Minami, Grandpa
Date of birth: 9 March 1993
Birthplace: Daegu, South Korea
Height: 1.74 metres (5'9")
Education: Daegu Taejeon Elementary School,
Gwaneum Middle School, Kangbuk High
School, Apgujeong High School, Global Cyber
University
Chinese zodiac: Rooster
Star sign: Pisces

EIGHT

MIN YOONGI/SUGA: THE SAVAGE SWAGMASTER

ARMY know there's more than one Suga. There's the rapper from Daegu who doesn't give a hoot what anyone thinks; there's cute Yoongi with a smile that breaks hearts; and there's Motionless Min, the sleepaholic who says that in the next life he wants to be a rock and do absolutely nothing. And don't forget producer Suga, so obsessed with finding the perfect beat he'll work anywhere – in airport departure lounges, TV studio waiting rooms, even toilet cubicles. One man, so many roles – no wonder he's always tired!

When ARMY write about Suga there's another word that is never far away: savage. He's brutal but awesome in word and deed. This is the guy who, when asked to describe himself, said, 'Min Suga, genius,' adding that no other words were needed. He's the rapper who, when the haters accused BTS of lip-syncing, deliberately stopped singing mid-song, and he's the mischievous member who breaks into English, just as RM finishes saying none of the others speak the language.

Min Yoongi, as he often likes to remind us, grew up in Daegu, in the North Gyeongsang Province. Men from the province are stereotyped as being temperamental and macho, and the dialect, in which he sometimes raps, can sound quite harsh to other Koreans. Like V, he spent some time being brought up by his grandmother and both seem to have had a tougher upbringing than the others. Suga has confessed that after debuting he went back to the dorm and sat staring blankly at the wall, amazed that a poor kid from Daegu could come so far.

> Suga has confessed that he was amazed that a poor kid from Daegu could come so far.

The fact that he had was thanks to his determination and his musical talent. The song 'First Love' tells how he learned to play the piano at elementary school and, although he fared well at his studies, it was music that captured his interest. And in 2005, when he discovered South Korean groups Stony Skunk and Epik High, he caught a love of hip-hop – and caught it bad. He still rates Epik High's song 'Fly' as an all-time favourite and credits their hopeful songs and refusal to compromise their musical credibility with inspiring and informing his musical aspirations. (In 2017, when Suga posted a picture of his Billboard Awards hotel pass, Epik High's Tablo gave it a treble thumbs-up, so it appears the admiration is now mutual.)

The teenage Min Yoongi set about finding out all he could about hip-hop. He taught himself how to operate music production software and by the age of seventeen he was working part-time at a recording studio, writing lyrics, and learning how to compose and arrange songs. He has recalled in interviews how he earned just enough for the bus to the studio and his food, sometimes having to walk home, which took two hours, if he'd spent too much on noodles.

Yoongi's hard work helped him make a name for himself in the Daegu music scene. He became a trusted source for 'beats' (backing tracks) for the city's rappers, produced their mixtapes and he even took a stage name, Gloss, and began rapping himself. In 2010, as part of the hip-hop crew D-Town, he produced and composed a song for a local festival. It commemorated the Gwangju Uprising, a 1980 demonstration in which hundreds of students were killed, and revealed the young songwriter's readiness to confront issues that others considered taboo.

> Yoongi's hard work helped him make a name for himself in the Daegu music scene.

Some months later, a flyer announcing that Bang Si-hyuk was holding a rap audition caught the eye of the high-school student. He passed the preliminary round, supposedly changing the beats to his own arrangement, but only came second in the final rap battle. Fortunately, Big Hit had been impressed by his production skills and took him on anyway, and when the winner, i11evn, left the company, Yoongi found himself in the group, the second of the final BTS line-up to join.

In interviews, Suga has revealed that although his brother supported him from the start, his parents were initially against him following a career in music, but once they came round they became enthusiastic fans, even calling him by his stage name. His father jokingly told a fan meeting that he didn't understand why ARMY liked Suga so much! At the 2016 HYYH Epilogue concert, on spotting his parents in the crowd, Suga fell to his knees and bowed to them, and in 2017 he bought his mother a restaurant in Daegu called Big Hearted Grandma's Blood Sausage Soup … which probably sounds better in Korean!

When Yoongi became a trainee idol he needed an idol name and he's given two reasons why he chose the name Suga. One relates to his love of basketball. Even as a trainee, he played every week. His position was shooting guard and 'Su Ga' is an abbreviation of the term. However, he's also said he was given the name Suga because his skin is very white compared to that of many Koreans and he's so sweet – especially when he smiles. Of course, ARMY tend to favour the second explanation!

Suga found being a trainee pretty hard-going. He tells of how much he disliked Bang Si-hyuk at the time and how he once walked out of practice to confront the boss and tell him he was leaving the group. Luckily, after a blazing row, he rejoined his friends in the rehearsal room. He also did part-time work to earn extra money while a trainee, including making deliveries by bike. After an accident on the road, he injured his shoulder. He hid his injury from the company and thought of going home. But when they found out, they offered to help him

BANGTAN BOMB

95z DANCE TIME WITH A BEAT APP

It's not always easy being a Bangtan. Just when you're trying to get a few minutes of valuable shut-eye, along come the 95 boys – Jimin and V – with energy to spare and mischief on their minds. With a Launchpad app playing beats and beeps, they shake it up right next to their sleeping brothers and manage not to get slapped! Who comes closest? Maybe Suga, if he could find the energy? Perhaps RM, if he wasn't so cool? Or maybe Jungkook, if the *maknae* wasn't supposed to show them respect?

financially and said they would wait until he had recovered and was able to resume his training.

That bond with the others helped him through those days. They call Suga 'Grandpa', as he's the one who changes the light bulbs, fixes doorknobs, mends the things RM breaks – and because he's frequently to be found having a nap! Though sometimes the serious one of the group who doesn't often take part in the younger members' games, Suga is respected and loved by the others. He has known and worked with RM since he joined Big Hit and, until moving to their latest plush apartment, had roomed with Jin since the beginning, refusing to countenance any idea of swapping, believing Jin to be the perfect roommate.

Suga's bond with Jungkook is the stuff of BTS legend. Suga himself has described him and the *maknae* as 'The Lamb Skewer Duo'. Ever since Suga introduced him to the meat-on-a-stick dish, it has been Jungkook's favourite food. Their joke was that he has asked Suga to go out and buy him some so often that they were going to set up a lamb kebab restaurant. This business idea came up frequently until 2017, when Jungkook told *ARMY* magazine that Suga's parents had told him it was an idea doomed to failure and Suga said he was looking at starting a furniture business instead!

Yoongi's real interest lies in technology: his very first vlog for BTS was a review of the digital controller he used for making beats. Later we became used to seeing him with a camera, and a hashtag appeared on Twitter which fans translated as 'Suga's sight'. It featured photos of BTS members, curiosities or places he had travelled to with the group. He famously wrote on one upload that it was fine to re-upload or edit it 'because I'm cool :)'.

Yoongi's individual personality won him a special place in ARMY affections when he demonstrated his practice 'chat-up line' in *American Hustle Life*: 'You like this chain? Three dollars.' They love his use of the word 'infires', his version of 'inspires', and the nonsense rap line 'Min Suga genius jjang jjang man boong boong', a phrase immortalized when it accompanied Suga's photo on Jimin's phone. Other cherished Suga moments include when he dressed in uniform and a black bob wig as an incredibly pretty schoolgirl character, Min Yoonji, in *Run BTS!*, and finally, ARMY have never forgotten the clip from a BTS signing event where one over-excited fangirl hilariously screams at Suga that he is a dangerous man and threatens to sue him for hurting her by being so gorgeous.

Because of his 'cool', reserved nature, Suga doesn't proclaim his love for ARMY as much as some of the others. He's Suga, he does it his own way. At a fan signing event back in 2014, he told ARMY that when he had made lots of money he would buy them meat. When, a

BANGTAN BOMB

BTS'S VOCAL DUET 'SOPE-ME' STAGE BEHIND THE SCENE

Suga and J-Hope – SOPE – are a pairing fans love to see together. Their occasional V-Live series 'Hwagae Marketplace' is often laugh-out-loud funny, their photos in matching 'SOPE' orange tracksuits for the 2016 *festa* was inspired, while this bomb, in which the rappers try out as vocalists, shows just how well they get on.

year later, he was asked when he would keep his promise he named 9 March 2018, his twenty-fifth birthday, which was then still three years in the future, as the date. True to his word, on that day he donated Korean beef to thirty-nine orphanages, not in his own name, but in the name of ARMY.

In January 2014, Suga's appendix burst while the band were doing promotions in Japan. He flew back to Korea for treatment, but a day after being discharged he was back in Tokyo for a fan showcase. During the event, the members were supposed to read from letters they had written to the fans. Jin, however, chose to read a letter he had written to Suga. He said how much he admired Suga for his determination to perform for ARMY despite being frail, but he also reminded him that it was okay to feel weak and that the other members of BTS would always look after him.

> In January 2014, Suga's appendix burst while the band were doing promotions in Japan ... A day after being discharged he was back in Tokyo for a fan showcase.

These were words that fans would remember in December 2015 when BTS announced they were cancelling a concert, again in Japan, because V and Suga were suffering from nausea. Although V was indeed physically ill on the day of the concert, Suga would later admit that, for him, it was a crippling anxiety that meant he had simply not been able to face the audience that night. It emerged that Suga has suffered with depression-related issues since his teenage years. Nevertheless he felt he had let the fans down in Japan. He admitted being unable to sleep, to waking in a cold sweat and being tearful about not performing. His tweets over the next few weeks revealed an artist at a low point. When the group finally had a break in their schedule, he had gone to the venue alone to try to feel the emotions of the fans he felt he had disappointed. With real honesty, he described himself as a weak person who acts as though he's strong, and he thanked ARMY for staying with him.

In August 2016, Suga released a free-to-download or stream mixtape, both titled and recorded under the name Agust D (backwards it reads DT Suga, with DT standing for Daegu Town). Produced entirely by Yoongi, in tracks such as 'Agust D' and 'Give It to Me' we get full-barrelled brag rap that defends his idol status, the first of these boasting of his 'tongue technology', a term ARMY will relish forever, but what the mixtape really allows Yoongi to do is tell his story.

BANGTAN BOMB

'뱁새' DANCE PRACTICE (흥 VERSION) – BTS (방탄소년단)

If you search for 'Bangtan Bomb festa dance practice 2016', you can watch Suga's hilarious reaction when he loses the rock, paper, scissors game during rehearsals for their 'Baepsae' dance for festa 2016. J-Hope usually performs the dance break when they perform the song, but now the 'honour' has fallen to the member who least likes the limelight. Suga, of course, brings his own, slightly different, approach to the dance solo. Elegant? No. Emotional? Not in the slightest. Amusing? You betcha!

Named after the buses he took to school in Daegu and Seoul, '724148' is about his journey from Daegu and the hardships of trainee life, working a part-time job in the morning, going to school in the day and training at night. And he really bares his soul, revealing the anxieties that seem capable of eating him up. This is especially true of 'The Last', where he speaks frankly of his continuing issues with obsessive compulsive disorder and depression, and of visits to psychiatrists.

The mixtape draws to a close with 'Tony Montana', which references the 'success doesn't equal happiness' story of the fictional gangster portrayed by Al Pacino in the 1983 film *Scarface*. It then finishes with the slow, soulful and very popular 'So Far Away', in which Yoongi tells of the courage needed to follow and see through your dream. Here the vocals are provided by Suran (Yoongi wrote her 2017 hit 'Wine').

With his production, songwriting, rapping and dancing skills, Suga has proved himself a massive talent and an integral part of BTS. He is also an honest, straight-talking guy with an underground rapper's heart and a sensitive side which together make up the savage and sweet Suga so beloved by ARMY.

NINE

BEAUTIFUL MOMENTS

omeback day dawned – and it looked like it could be the most crucial comeback of the boys' careers. They wanted that music-show win so much. It was mentioned in so many of the interviews they did in spring 2015 and was even brought up in the skit on their forthcoming album. It was easier said than done, though. There were so many popular K-pop artists on the scene. They needed to produce something very special.

The new mini-album, *The Most Beautiful Moment in Life, Part 1*, was announced with the now familiar teasers for the end of April 2015. The trailer was once again a rap, but this time from Suga not RM, and with it was a beautiful Japanese-style animation featuring a young man hiding from the realities of life as he played alone on the basketball court. It ended with lyrics which explained that, even in times of hardship, happiness can be found in 'beautiful moments'.

RM thought long and hard about the theme that would cover this and the next release, before choosing the Chinese phrase *Hwa yang yeon hwa* (sometimes abbreviated to HYYH) to sum up the philosophy behind the album. The phrase is usually interpreted as 'the age of blossoms', a metaphor for the passing of youth, beauty and love, but, in keeping with BTS's mission to talk directly about the anxieties and problems of the young, the group opted for a slightly different translation for their album title: 'The most beautiful moment in life'.

Later, during live performances, RM elaborated on the theme, emphasizing how the young must cherish their moments of joy and beauty, even though they may be struggling in school, in a job, with their parents or in a relationship. The concert DVD English subtitles translate his words as: 'If you know and feel this moment truthfully with the heart, and that you're ready to accept the moment, then from the time when you're born, the entire life can be beautiful.'

> RM elaborated on the theme, emphasizing how the young must cherish their moments of joy and beauty, even though they may be struggling.

Shortly after the trailer came the new concept photos. A set was revealed for each of the two album designs – a pink version and a white version. The first version contrasted splashes of colour in the boys' clothes, the green grass and flowers, and the sakura trees of Gyeongju National Park with their sombre mood. The second set, this time shot in black and white, reflected a similar mood, but was taken at Yeongdeok on the Sea of Japan with a wintery seaside backdrop.

On 29 April 2015, before the album and video drop at midnight, BTS appeared on *Starcast* in their own hour-long live show, called 'I Need U BTS on Air' (it's still available to view on V-Live), where they talked about the photoshoot and the album, and performed a stunning 'slow jam' live version of 'I Need U'. Seeing them laughing and joking together in such a carefree way made the sombre posing seem almost unbelievable but, as we were about to discover, as well as singing and dancing superbly, these boys were also pretty good actors.

There was no dancing in the 'I Need U' music video, just a dark,

dark story. It's actually so dark that the original video was re-edited, because it contained scenes that could shock or upset younger viewers (it was later uploaded with a 19+ warning by the title). It takes the idea of the fragility of youth to a grim conclusion: a descent into violence, overdosing on pills and even hints of suicide. The frustrations of 'Danger' are nothing compared to the extremes depicted here, as each of the group are given their individual stories, all with a theme of desperation and despair.

Shot through a blue filter, the melancholic scenes really give the boys the chance to play a role – Jimin burns letters as he sits in the bath, Jungkook is set upon by thugs, V reacts violently to his abusive father – and they're very believable. The images are laden with symbolism about leaving childhood behind and plummeting self-esteem, so it's unsurprising that ARMY continue to come up with theories about the meaning of the video.

The atmosphere of loneliness contrasts perfectly with clips of the group as a whole. Here they are not alone, but laughing, hugging, play-fighting and enjoying each other's company. Dressed in English-style casual wear – a Fred Perry polo shirt for Jimin, punk band T-shirt for V, check shirt with braces for RM, and bomber jacket and white tee for Suga – they come across as ordinary lads out having fun.

The video did its job. Within hours #Ineedu was trending across social media and the stage was set for the mini-album release. The pink and white versions of the CD were both packaged with an exquisite 120-page photobook full of even more pictures from both the flower and the seaside photoshoots, as well as the usual random member photo and a group picture.

Suga's forceful rap from the trailer serves as the album's intro. It's a passionate rant against the voices of self-doubt, which is driven by the beat of the bouncing basketball and heightened by the sound of sneakers squeaking on the court. This leads straight into the single, 'I Need U', which sets the electro-pop sound and emotional intensity levels for the rest of the album and returns to the familiar theme of longing for a love that has ended. This, however, is a more mature reflection on the topic. They are no longer boys in 'luv'; this is serious and for the first time they are prepared to use the word 'love'.

Those who discovered BTS at this point may not have quite appreciated that this was when it all came together. The transitions between singers and rappers are so much smoother. They move further away from hip-hop and towards a softer pop style, but they keep the beat alive. It isn't an imitation of US rap and it isn't Korean hip-hop or pure K-pop. They were forging a sound which was truly their own and 'I Need U' was their most complete single yet.

However, anyone missing the dance element on the music video didn't have to wait long. Just a few days after release, Big Hit put out a dance practice video for the song. This was more subtle than many of their dances and the general effect is of waves of movement until the chorus, when that amazing sharp and angular dance action comes to the fore. The excitement heightened in anticipation of the music-show promotions to come.

> They were forging a sound which was truly their own and 'I Need U' was their most complete single yet.

Track three, 'Hold Me Tight', marked V's songwriting debut. Having watched the rap line at work for such a long time, he had waited patiently before emerging with this gentle piano and synth love song. The revealing 'Skit: Expectation!' follows, in which the band discuss their hopes for the album or, indeed, whether they dare hope at all.

This shows the group's insecurity; that they really want to believe they have a chance of success, but are held back by modesty or perhaps a lack of real self-belief. There was, however, a lovely interview with Jin on the TV show *Pops in Seoul* in which he claimed he knew 'I Need U' would be a hit, because whenever J-Hope says something will be a flop, it does well, and J-Hope had predicted disappointing results for the new single!

'Welcome. First time with BTS?' asks RM, greeting the ever-growing new recruits to ARMY, at the beginning of 'Dope'. The energy returns in this, track five of the album, and with it comes the most popular song BTS had recorded to date. *Billboard*'s Jeff Benjamin, one of the group's earliest mainstream champions in the US, praised the song's 'aggressive lyrics, party-ready production and exotic horn-laden breakdown'. America was starting to take notice of BTS. And how could it not? In a really upbeat track, BTS parade their ability to merge a string synth sound, a jazzy break and a pounding beat as they sing about defeating their critics and celebrating their success. It's as if, despite their modest expectations, they knew this was going to work all along.

What you want at this point is a feel-good foot-stomper and along comes 'Boyz with Fun', which is exactly that. Once they performed this good-time bop on music shows it became a firm live favourite with its relatively easy to imitate choreography and the crowd-pleasing tradition in which V invents a move the others have to copy.

'Boyz with Fun' and the next track, 'Converse High', had both been previewed in the concerts at Seoul's Olympic Hall in March. The subject of the latter, written by RM, was familiar to those who had heard him interviewed about his ideal type: he likes a girl who wears red Converse trainers. In this smooth, R&B-infused song he manages to convince the rest of the band of the excellence of his preferred make of footwear – except (of course) for Suga, who won't be told, and has his own verse dissing the brand!

In spring 2015 the boys had finally moved dorms. They originally shared a small dorm with all seven of them sleeping in one room, but with their success they had moved to a bigger, three-bedroom dorm where Jin and Suga shared one space, RM and Jungkook another, and J-Hope, Jimin and V a third. So in the next song, 'Move', a light hip-hop-with-guitars track, they talk about their change of dorms, their memories – happy and sad – of the last place, and use moving as a metaphor for going up the rankings as idols.

The ninth and final track, 'Outro: Love Is Not Over', continues the tradition of the vocal line closing the album. This piano-accompanied ballad was Jin and Jungkook's opportunity to shine in the songwriting department and they did just that, with a beautiful, soul-wrenching denial of the end of a romance.

BANGTAN BOMB

UP DOWN UP UP DOWN (BY EXID)

More green room goofing around and this time J-Hope and Jimin lead a spontaneous parody of 'Up and Down' by girl group EXID. This one's got over 5 million views, possibly in appreciation of the 'sexy dancing' on show, perhaps because it's the source of a celebrated Jimin face-pull, or maybe because it's a dance they later repeat on *Weekly Idol*.

From the outset, BTS have attempted to create a unique relationship with their fans through social network sites and YouTube. From summer 2015, although the bombs, dance practices and other videos continued to be uploaded to YouTube, other BTS videos appeared on the newly launched V-Live. This app allows K-pop groups to post live and recorded videos (with English translations) and even chat to their fans in real time.

The first BTS series that appeared on the V-Live app consisted of five ten-minute episodes called *BTS Bokbulbok*. The title translates as *Lucky Draw* or *Lucky or Not* and the group pick a random game – it could be a boxing video game, mini table tennis or cup stacking – to play in their dance studio. Check out the first episode where they play charades, with Jungkook, Jin and Jimin being kangaroos, or episode three in which a blindfolded V scoots around the dancefloor in a hilarious round of hide-and-seek.

In August 2015, V-Live began broadcasting a fun music-based series called *BTS Gayo*. In the eight episodes (or 'tracks' as they're called here) the challenges see them perform girl-group dances or try to recognize members' impressions of other K-pop singers. ARMY especially love track two, where the boys re-enact romantic scenes from Korean movies, and track six, where a quest to find the worst dancer in BTS ends in a fabulous impromptu dance battle between Suga and J-Hope.

Another V-Live series, *Run BTS!*, saw the boys freed from the studio, and given even more scope for games, challenges and activities. If you wonder whether J-Hope ever stops smiling, then watch him on the rollercoaster when they all visit a theme park in episode three. And, if you believe they're tough guys, just watch them sweat on the elevator to the bungee jump in episode nine!

V-Live would become an important outlet for BTS. Individual members had their own live shows such as 'Eat Jin', Suga and J-Hope's 'Hwagae Marketplace', J-Hope's 'Hope on the Street' and Jimin and V's 'What are the 95z Doing?'. The group also regularly broadcast live on the app, whether backstage at awards ceremonies, in the dressing room before TV variety shows, on every member's birthday, and before and even after concerts all around the world.

Meanwhile, BTS hadn't forgotten the importance of television. With the video for 'I Need U' reaching 1 million views in sixteen hours and number five in the Gaon charts, and the mini-album going in at number two, they prepared their stages for the Korean TV music shows. Could they finally take that elusive show victory?

J-HOPE

FACT FILE

Name: Jung Hoseok
Nicknames: J-Hope, Hobi, Horse, Smile Hoya
Date of birth: 18 February 1994
Birthplace: Gwangju, South Korea
Height: 1.77 metres (5'10")
Education: Ilgok Middle School, Kukje High School, Global Cyber University
Chinese zodiac: Dog
Star sign: Aquarius

TEN

JUNG HOSEOK/J-HOPE: THE SUNSHINE OF BTS

Even if you're new to BTS, J-Hope is easy to spot in any group interview. He'll be the one with the beaming smile. What if a few of them are smiling? No worries. Wait a minute or so and one of them will start whooping, waving or, if you're lucky, dancing. That'll be J-Hope.

Right from debut, J-Hope's energy and exuberance has driven BTS. In interviews, vlogs, Bangtan bombs and performances, his good nature is a given. In a *festa* conversation Suga once suggested that this wasn't the case when they were trainees and that it was the 'Hope' name that took Hoseok into optimism overdrive. Whether that's true or not, J-Hope is proud to be BTS's ray of sunshine, often introducing himself by saying, 'I'm your hope, I'm your angel.'

Of course, J-Hope is so much more than a happy mascot for BTS. He takes his place on the rap line, has contributed to the writing and production of over fifty BTS tracks and is the main dancer. It is J-Hope who takes the lead in dance rehearsals, helping the others master the steps in the long practice sessions. In fact, BTS choreographer Song Seongdeuk has commented on J-Hope's commitment and sense of

Jimin has noted how strict the usually soft-hearted J-Hope becomes when teaching dance.

duty in the way he guides the other members, while Jimin has noted how strict the usually soft-hearted J-Hope becomes when teaching dance.

Unlike some others in the group, J-Hope arrived at Big Hit as an accomplished dancer. He had been dancing since he was at elementary school, and he recalled his thrill at the reaction he received when he performed on stage in a talent competition there. The love of music and expressing himself through dance would never leave him.

Young Hoseok and his older sister, Jung Dawon (who now has a clothing line called 'Mejiwoo'), grew up in a loving family in Gwangju, a city in the south-west corner of South Korea. When an early enthusiasm for tennis faded, inspired by dance videos he saw a perfect outlet for his passion for music and performance. In middle school, he kept up his studies, but was already building a reputation among his friends for his dancing ability, and even won a national dance competition.

At high school, he claims to have been well behaved, but he probably had little choice – his father was a literature teacher there. He didn't achieve particularly high grades, but he did excel at hip-hop-style popping. By fifteen he was learning dance at an academy, performing regularly with a local street dance team called Neuron, and even auditioned for JYP Entertainment company. V later recalled that when BTS debuted, his friends asked if J-Hope was that dancer from the academy in Gwangju (at that time his stage name had been 'Smile Hoya'). 'That's how famous he was,' V concluded.

According to J-Hope, it was his love of dance and his willingness to work hard that brought him to Big Hit's attention. Legend has it that after a Big Hit dance video audition in his home town, when staff returned several hours later to pack up they found him still hard at work practising, so word went back to Seoul that here was one dedicated talent.

In December 2010, J-Hope became the third of the final BTS line-up to sign with Big Hit. He arrived in the dorm on Christmas Eve and was soon hit by the reality of trainee life: long hours of intense practice and sleeping in the dorm. It was Suga who looked after him in those tough early days, even turning up with chicken when J-Hope faced a New Year's Eve alone in the dorm.

Our man took the 'J' from his name Jung and added 'Hope' because he wanted to be the optimistic member of the group, which he's certainly succeeded at being. He was not only recruited as a dancer, but as one of the vocal line, too, and it wasn't until V joined the company six months later as a vocalist that J-Hope switched to the rap line. This was a new skill for him, but he worked diligently with the company staff and coaches to develop his own distinct style.

Like all the members, J-Hope found the trainee period arduous and became frustrated waiting for debut day. In the *Burn the Stage* documentary, the group discuss the time when he decided to leave the group. We hear how Jungkook sobbed and RM talked to Big Hit to persuade him to stay. He says he only returned because he trusted that the group would eventually find success.

ARMY are so grateful that he did. Hobi, as they sometimes call him, has astonished with his performances on so many occasions. His amazing dance skills stole the stage in the MAMA battles in 2014 and 2015, and his solo display in 'Boy Meets Evil' just takes your breath away. As the main dancer, he's often credited for his part in creating and interpreting the complex choreography BTS are given, and in a V-Live special for 'DNA', V said J-Hope could do the trickiest choreography

J-Hope could do the trickiest choreography they'd ever attempted in just ten minutes.

they'd ever attempted in just ten minutes.

Not that he is just a dancer. His smooth and sometimes incredibly fast rap style provides a contrast to the rougher tones of RM and Suga. Listen to 'Whalien 52', 'Ma City', 'Cypher Pt. 3: Killer', 'Let Me Know' or 'Boy Meets Evil' and it's hard to believe he's a rap convert. And in later tracks such as 'Rain', 'Tomorrow' and especially his ode to his mother, 'Mama', when he does sing he shows exactly why he was originally picked for the vocal line.

J-Hope's love of dance inspired his V-Live videos 'Hope on the Street' (now viewable on YouTube). These feature J-Hope dancing and giving dance tips to viewers, but mainly just having a good time. He's joined by Jungkook in one episode and in another Jimin arrives on a hoverboard and, eventually, V turns up on a bike and they have some freestyle fun.

Born in 1994, Hobi forms a natural bridge between the older members and the 95 line. Open and good-humoured, he seems to get along effortlessly with the rest of the group. It's been noted that when everyone else has failed, he's the one who can always get Suga laughing, and their SOPE friendship is clear in the Hwagae Market vlogs, the SOPE-ME duet and the fab orange tracksuits.

The other obvious connection is with Jimin as the 95-liner was the first to bond with him, helped by the time they spent at dance practice together. J-Hope and Jimin also room together, initially along with V, but even when they moved into their luxury apartment and everyone got their own room, Jimin and J-Hope chose to share the largest of the rooms. J-Hope has said, 'I'm the older one and Jimin really does listen to me. We don't usually say this to each other face to face, but

I'm always grateful to him.' Jimin, by turn, is thankful that J-Hope falls asleep instantly as soon as he gets into bed and he trusts his *hyung* so much that he offered him sole responsibility for cleaning the room. J-Hope declined the offer!

Jimin has also said that J-Hope can make friends with anyone and the long list of his friends from the K-pop world backs this up. Among them,

> J-Hope can make friends with anyone.

Ravi from VIXX, Hyerin from EXID, Hyungwon of Monsta X, Ladies' Code's Zuny, B.A.P's Zelo and BIGSTAR's Sunghak are all close to Hobi. In March 2018, Jo Kwon from 2PM posted pictures of him and J-Hope together, saying he was so proud of how far his friend had come since they first met six years ago when pre-debut J-Hope rapped and danced on the video for Jo Kwon's solo track, 'Animal'.

His charisma, caring nature and exuberance (not to mention his ability to pull the most amazing facial expressions) have naturally endeared him to BTS fans, too. In the early variety shows when the other members were often a little reserved, J-Hope was always willing to put himself out there. Few can forget the 2015 episode of *Yaman TV* when he performed a jaw-dropping dance medley of girl-group choreographies, most impressively of Red Velvet's 'Ice Cream Cake'. Go find it now – and while you are looking you might just come across the word 'snake'.

BTS's 2015 summer package (a video photoshoot released as a DVD) included a trip to the zoo, where J-Hope was introduced to a particularly large snake. As it's draped around his shoulders, he's obviously terrified, but his reaction is very funny – and indeed became a favourite fan meme. It soon became clear that this was just one of his fears. In various *Run BTS!* episodes he has a similar reaction to riding a rollercoaster and bungee-jumping, but full marks to him for being brave enough to put himself through such ordeals just so the fans can be entertained with the hysterical consequences!

When interviewed about the snake incident on SBS Asia, J-Hope came out with the classic phrase, 'I hate snakeu!' Now, he's no fool, and can speak a number of languages (particularly Japanese), but his own brand of English has produced some moments that ARMY cherish. Of course, he was the instigator of the whole 'Jimin's got no jams' conversation, with his instruction to 'All English speakeu', and that also produced gems such as 'Oh my hearteu is, my hearteu is ...' and 'Oh Jimin is very no fun!'

J-Hope is also known for his promise to produce a mixtape. Over the years the idea has progressed from 'dream' to 'on my 2017 to-do list' to 'working on it' and some believed it would never happen, but it just turned out to be the longest teaser in history, because on 1 March 2018 *Hope World* was dropped – and boy was it worth waiting for!

BANGTAN BOMB

J-HOPE VS 95z

Don't be fooled by the title. It's not a dance-off and it isn't a singing challenge. This is just what happens when you wake a sleeping ray of sunshine. J-Hope is the one senior member who the 95 line know they can rely on for a bit of fun – but just how far can they push him? Quite far, as it turns out in this charming caper.

The cartoon-like, vibrantly coloured cover sets the tone immediately and the 'hixtape', as *Hope World* was tagged by ARMY, features seven tracks that span pop, tropical, EDM, trap and hard rap (or as hard as J-Hope goes, with BTS producer Supreme Boi adding some grit to one number), all adorned with a sweetly sung J-Hope take on the world. There's no intro here, just the title track 'Hope World', a dance number that uses his favourite book from childhood, Jules Verne's *Twenty Thousand Leagues Under the Sea*, to introduce him and his perspective on life.

'Daydream' is the first of the lead tracks. The vivid, heightened-colour video is a perfect match for the funky, bounce-along track and a real gift for J-Hope fans, featuring him in all his guises from sleepy Hobi to rapper to sharp-suited singer. The other lead track, 'Airplane', accompanied by a music video featuring a more thoughtful J-Hope, has a much more mellow vibe as he reflects on how his life has panned out. He told *Time* magazine, 'I was sitting in an airplane when I was writing these verses, a first-class seat no less, and it dawned on me that I was living the glorious life I'd only dreamed about when I was young and had somehow gotten used to now. But then and now, I'm still the same person, the same J-Hope.'

The mixtape is 100 per cent J-Hope, and you can feel his warmth and personality in every track. Throughout, we can feel the idea of a guy who finds enjoyment in the moment, but also someone who is sensitive to the struggles and trouble of others. He is also never far from BTS, admitting his success is part of a group achievement; they are even present in the backing chants of 'Airplane'.

The positive vibe, catchy melodies and lyrical depth of *Hope World* seemed to surprise even J-Hope's biggest fans. It went to number one in the iTunes charts in over seventy countries and broke the top forty in the Billboard 200. Meanwhile, the 'Daydream' video amassed 20 million views on YouTube in just a few days.

Who wouldn't delight in such a triumph? Those who have followed BTS over the years have seen his development as a rapper, dancer and vocalist, but have also seen what J-Hope has given to the group. While as a friend he is caring and affectionate, as a BTS member he provides energy, excitement and entertainment. He truly is as he claims: the sunshine of the group, our hope and our angel.

ELEVEN

ALL AROUND THE WORLD

Different Korean music shows have slightly different ways of calculating their weekly winners, but all follow a generally similar format. They take into consideration digital downloads, music video views, experts' reviews and album sales to select the nominees, and then allow live votes to contribute to the result. In the case of *The Show Choice*, 15 per cent of the points come from live voting. Up against the previous week's winners EXID and Block B sub-unit BASTARZ, BTS faced a huge challenge; they needed their fans to respond. And ARMY did – magnificently.

'The 27th The Show Choice was won by BTS!! Congratulations on winning your first music show #1! We hope you continue to be the best!! Congratulations to ARMY, too!' That tweet was sent out by SBS MTV's *The Show Choice* on the evening of 5 May 2015, confirming what many had already found out: BTS had done it. 'I Need U' had won them their first show number one.

Two days later, they won again. This time on *M Countdown* and again, the following day, at *Music Bank*, to their sheer disbelief. After eight days they had won a total of five shows, including returning to win *The Show Choice* for a second time.

With the album reaching number one in the weekly Gaon chart,

BANGTAN BOMB

AFTER M!COUNTDOWN 1ST PLACE T-T

Just in case it wasn't clear what achieving that winning position meant to them, here's the boys' reaction after their second win. With red-smudged lips, after they have fulfilled a promise to perform their encore in lipstick if they win, they jump around, gush, hug, stare in disbelief and, in the case of Jimin, find a quiet corner in which to have a little cry. Beautiful.

and the group performing in May at Dream 2015, the Seoul World Cup Stadium K-pop festival, which only invites the very best acts, naturally they were all on top of the world. Fittingly, it was the perfect time to celebrate, with their second *festa* (their debut anniversary celebrations – keep up!) coming in June. This time, with ARMY three times bigger than last year, they embarked on a two-week bonding session with the fans who had delivered them the big prize.

The *festa* began with a fabulous new track on YouTube, 'Hug Me', a sensitive ballad cover song performed by V with an added rap from J-Hope. Once again, they all got together to chat for an hour-long radio broadcast that included a hilarious version of 'I Need U' in which the rap line and the vocal line swapped parts, and a segment where they chose their ambition for the coming year. While Jimin wanted them to play an even bigger stadium, V dreamed of them making a cycling trip together, RM suggested a group vacation, and Jungkook had plans for then all to learn *Wing Chun Gyeon*, a Chinese martial art.

Other *festa* festivities saw them post a series of 'real family pictures' on Facebook. Some showed them all deliberately looking stiff and awkward with forced smiles as they posed in matching suits, while others featured J-Hope, Jimin, Jin and Jungkook standing behind one another in a typical dorky 'brothers' pose. And the treats didn't finish there. Two special new dance practices were uploaded on YouTube. The first was 'War of Hormone' (see Bangtan bomb overleaf) and the second a version of 'Blanket Kick' with the boys having fun going full-on *aegyo* – acting shy and cute.

While ARMY were still reeling from *festa*, along came the release of 'Dope' as a single and an accompanying music video. In August 2017, this would become the first BTS video to pass 200 million views, but in June 2015 it did the job of keeping up the BTS profile. The video is vintage Bangtan, beautifully filmed in a one-camera continuous shoot. The boys look great in their fantasy costumes – RM as a concierge, J-Hope a racing-car driver, Jungkook a police officer, Suga (now sporting a blond look) a naval officer, V a manga comic Detective Conan, Jin a doctor and Jimin (whose hair colour J-Hope calls strawberry ice-cream) a businessman. And the choreography is phenomenal. It is the first time they have worked with the legendary Keone Madrid and it is their most intense, powerful and synchronized routine yet.

As they promoted the single, the costumes became wonderfully random: J-Hope appeared as a tennis player, Jin as an aircraft pilot, Jungkook as an engineer, Suga as a secret agent, or they could all appear together in military uniform. It was as if they were saying, 'We can be anything we want to be.' And as the video picked up views, something else was happening, too: the song reached number three in the Billboard World Charts. It was the best-performing BTS single in this category so far.

The USA wasn't the only English-speaking country where ARMY was growing rapidly. In mid-July BTS took their Red Bullet to Australia, where concerts in Sydney and Melbourne had sold out in minutes. In Australia, BTS seemed chilled. On the Australian music show *SBS Pop Asia* they named their favourite Australian animals, impersonated each other (as well as RM doing a great Marge Simpson impression) and even tried some of the nation's favourite spread, Vegemite. Jin seemed to like it, but for once J-Hope wasn't smiling!

As was becoming the norm, long queues formed early on the day before each concert Down Under. It was worth the wait. The opening video – here a classroom registration of the members, all of whom were absent – produced feverish excitement, and a crescendo of screams, yells, fan chants and waving light sticks greeted the boys' appearance

BANGTAN BOMB

'호르몬전쟁' DANCE PERFORMANCE (REAL WAR VER.)

Twenty million-plus views don't lie. This second *festa* gift is a massive ARMY favourite. It's the 'War of Hormone' choreography, but not as we know it. This is the 'boys go crazy' version, which they refer to as 'real war', and they're out to have as much fun as possible. It doesn't matter who your bias is, they all have their moments here – but it's hard to ignore V, who is enjoying himself way beyond the legal limit!

on stage. In a breathless opening medley they played 'N.O', 'We Are Bulletproof Pt. 2', 'We On' and 'Hip Hop Lover', before slowing the pace with 'Let Me Know' and 'Rain'.

Although almost drowned out by the audience, the songs were spot on and the dances were slick. They were punctuated by various members trying out their English. As the concerts progressed through a twenty-four-song, two-hour set, various surprises ensued. The boys introduced a karaoke section for fans to sing along to 'Miss Right' and 'I Like It', and they played rock, paper, scissors to determine who had to perform the cute dance to K-pop classic 'The Gwiyomi Song'. The shows came to a close with 'I Need U' and 'Boy in Luv', but there was no way these Aussie – or any other – fans were letting them go.

The encore began with another video, this time of the pre-debut Bangtan Boys hard at work, and then they performed 'Dope' live for the first time, before ending on the high-energy 'Boyz with Fun' and 'Rise of Bangtan'. In Sydney, the boys left the stage one by one – Jimin staying until last, when another band member had to return to drag him off. The audience and the band were euphoric, but completely drained.

And so the Red Bullet sped on. BTS were returning to the US. That meant In-N-Out, Shake Shack, hot dogs, doughnuts and Korean food just as good as at home – oh, and the small matter of ARMY impatient to see their heroes. To prove it, they snaffled up the 12,500 show tickets in minutes.

As ARMY brought Times Square to a standstill with a flash mob dance, the group flew in to New York for the first ever time to perform on 16 July 2015 at the Best Buy Theater. They got the customary rapturous

ARMY brought Times Square to a standstill with a flash mob dance.

reception and fans raised a banner reading, in Korean, 'Just One Day with BTS', which made the boys all smile. However, the night was not without controversy. After coming back for an encore, the group played just one more number and then left suddenly. Even worse, they cancelled the after-show hi-touch event as well. It appeared there were safety concerns after threats had been made to the group on social media, and, although these proved to be groundless, the BTS management felt they couldn't take any chances.

Nevertheless, the show left an impression for the right reasons on those who had seen it. *Billboard*'s review admired how the group, unlike other K-pop acts, hadn't stuck to the synchronized dances, but had freestyled from as early as the third song. Jeff Benjamin, the publication's K-pop specialist, remarked how natural, casual and fun this had made the show feel.

The tour continued to Dallas on 18 July and Chicago on 24 July, before landing the boys back in LA on 26 July at the 2,300-seat venue Club Nokia. There, Suga told the crowd that LA was his 'second home' and they brought the house down once again. Watching and waiting for them afterwards was Tony, their mentor from *American Hustle Life*. He celebrated by posting a photo of his reunion with the band on Instagram and Twitter with the legend 'Great show, lil' bros killed it tonight at Club Nokia.'

Like all crowds on the Red Bullet tour, those in LA were excited and exuberant, but something about the fans had changed. A year ago, when they had played in the City of Angels at their 'secret' *American Hustle Life* concert or at KCON, the boys had performed to a largely Korean-American audience. In 2015, although Korean-Americans were still out in force, there was a diverse ethnic mix and even some guys and older fans! No longer niche, BTS were heading mainstream.

Down in Central and South America, the locals were ahead of the game and the continent had already taken K-pop to its heart. Exactly what caused the *hallyu*, or 'Korean wave', to take such a hold there has been the subject of much debate. Of course, as in other regions of the world, fans in South America could watch an enormous volume of high-quality material – songs, shows, videos – online, but they were now very grateful that BTS, live and in person, were coming their way.

From the end of July to early August there were concerts in Mexico, Chile and Brazil, at the biggest venues they had played outside Japan, and people flocked to the shows, not just from those countries, but from adjacent nations such as Argentina, Peru and Colombia. The enthusiasm of the fans certainly made an impression on the boys. Jungkook picked the concert in São Paolo as one of the highlights of the tour, while RM spoke of Brazilian and Chilean ARMY as the most passionate BTS fans in the world.

Eventually, though, it was time to head home. The Red Bullet tour was nearly over, with just two concerts in Thailand and Hong Kong remaining. In eleven months, BTS had played to packed, sold-out venues in fourteen different countries over five continents. There was no stopping them now.

JIMIN

FACT FILE

Name: Park Jimin
Nicknames: Jimin, Jiminie, Little Prince, Chim Chim, Dooly, Mochi, *Manggae*, Ddochi
Date of birth: 13 October 1995
Birthplace: Busan, South Korea
Height: 1.73 metres (5'8")
Education: Heodang Elementary School, Yoonsan Middle School, Busan High School of Arts, Korean Arts High School, Global Cyber University
Chinese zodiac: Pig
Star sign: Libra

TWELVE

PARK JIMIN: HE'S GOT JAMS!

Park Jimin was the last piece of the BTS jigsaw. Brought in just months before the BTS line-up was confirmed, he had thrilling dance skills, a singing voice with such potential and the looks of an angel. And yet there were some at Big Hit who didn't think this piece of the jigsaw fitted. At the *Love Yourself: Her* showcase, he revealed that in his short time as a trainee he was kicked off the team eight times (V reckons it was more like fifteen!), and Suga seems to think he was almost left out on the day before their debut – but just try to imagine a BTS without Jimin.

Not only are his vocals now seen as an essential ingredient of BTS songs and his dancing as a highlight of video and stage performances, he is also one of the most fun and playful members of the group. He frequently posts to BTS social media accounts, updating ARMY with messages, photos and videos, and although RM may have famously implied that Jimin was no fun when he pronounced that Jimin's 'got no jams', every ARMY knows that in fact Jimin has jams to spare.

Jimin describes his childhood in the South Korean port city of Busan as happy. Home life was spent having fun with his brother, who is only a couple of years younger, as they played games and watched movies together. He sounds such a boy as he remembers wanting to be a chef, a pirate or the driver of the space train *Galaxy Express 999*. He was the same happy-go-lucky character at school, enjoying his studies and getting on with all his classmates.

He says he fell in love with dancing in his early teens, while in the second year of middle school. Inspired by Korean pop superstar Rain, he set his sights on becoming an idol. He spent more and more time at the dance academy after school and by the time he was to choose a high school, his mind was made up. He would go to Busan High School of Arts and major in modern dance. Then, in the spring of 2012, on the advice of his middle-school dance teacher, he tried out for Big Hit.

'It was my first ever audition so my hands were shaking.'

In a 2013 interview with *Cuvism* magazine, Jimin recalled, 'It was my first ever audition so my hands were shaking a lot when I opened the door. I also remember that my voice shook a lot while singing, but because I started dancing at a young age, I danced very confidently. I sang "I Have a Lover". RM has teased him about this, because at the time it was the most popular karaoke song among middle-schoolers, but Jimin says at that point he hadn't learned how to sing and just didn't have a clue what to pick.

By May of that year he was on his way to Seoul to become a trainee. Jimin remembers J-Hope being the first person he met, and recalls that he was welcomed into the dorm with the words, 'Let's work hard together!' And he would soon find out just what hard work was. Having joined Big Hit, Jimin transferred to a school in Seoul and found himself at the same high school as V, the two of them leaving for it together in the morning in their uniforms (Jimin wore V's actual uniform in the

'Graduation Song' video). Although they were in different classes, V helped out his shy new friend by getting his classmates to talk to him.

Suga would recall that his first impression of Jimin was that he must be an excellent singer or dancer because this slightly overweight boy in thick glasses certainly wasn't a visual. But he would soon see another facet of the then sixteen-year-old: determination. Jimin would do a full day at school, practise until three or four in the morning and have a few hours' sleep before getting up to do an hour's singing and then setting off for school again.

As tough as it was, Jimin valued his trainee time. Those around him soon noted his perfectionism and how eager he was to improve. He also appreciated spending time and eating with the other trainees. He says he still carries an amusement park admission ticket in his wallet, a souvenir of one of their first trips out together.

> Those around him soon noted his perfectionism and how eager he was to improve.

When doubts arose about him before debut, it was the rest of the members who seem to have argued to keep Jimin in the group, and he says that in the darker days it was their confidence in him that drove him to work harder and believe in himself. He even had the confidence, with the backing of the other members, to turn down the stage names Big Hit suggested for him, which included Baby J and Young Kid. He said he was hoping for something better, so instead plumped to use his own name.

By the time debut day arrived, Jimin had the star dance role: running across the others' backs. It was a real thrill, but nerve-racking for him as he didn't want to kick his friends too hard. And then came the transformed 'chocolate abs', the toned stomach muscles that look like the divided parts of a chocolate bar (a 'six pack'). At first, the naturally shy Jimin was embarrassed at showing off his ripped torso on the dance floor, but he's also someone who likes to please his audience and, as early as the first *festa*, J-Hope revealed that when Jimin saw the reaction he was getting from flashing his abs, his shyness disappeared pretty quickly! When they decided he would tear his shirt off at the 2014 MAMAs performance, his determination kicked in again and he began exercising even more, visiting the gym before going to sleep even when they were on tour in Asia.

> When Jimin saw the reaction he was getting from flashing his abs, his shyness disappeared.

Jimin's looks have changed more than those of any other member in BTS's five-year rise to superstardom. This was the chubby-cheeked boy who was nicknamed Ddochi by his middle-school friends after a cartoon ostrich who puffs his cheeks out, and *manggae* (soft rice cakes) by ARMY, who loved his squishy face, but when the 'Blood, Sweat & Tears' video was released, a different Jimin emerged. Through intense dieting, he had lost the puppy features. He's a guy who cares about his looks – and he's not the only one.

Whether it is his soft, thick lips that produce the perfect pout and smile, his large eyes that take so well to the smoky eyeliner look, or his fluffy hair that induced gasps when he dyed it candy-floss pink, Jimin has what it takes to excite an audience. He also knows how to work a crowd from the stage. Tony Jones, his mentor in *American Hustle Life* and the first to name him Chim Chim, nailed it in an interview with the MoonROK website when he said, 'When he's performing and winking, he's got all that fan service down. His attitude is so positive. I'd say charming ... and he just knows how to give the crowd what they want.' Just watch videos of him on stage as he shrugs his shirt off his shoulders and you'll understand how Jimin always has the audience in the palm of his hand.

It helps that Jimin is a pretty amazing dancer. Having studied modern dance at high school, when he joined Big Hit he switched to street dance, but perhaps it's that contemporary dance background that adds an elegant quality to BTS's hip-hop style. Just watch his blindfolded dance in 'Boy Meets Evil' at MAMA 2016, his incredible solo to 'Butterfly' or his balletic moves alongside Twice's Mina and Momo in the end-of-year TV special *SBS Gayo Daejun* in 2016. For such a shy boy, Jimin really comes alive when he performs. It has now reached the point where the others joke that in the live shows he always seems to hog centre-stage!

Jimin definitely has his self-doubts, though. During the promotion of *Wings*, he explained that the high notes in 'Lie' made it difficult for

BANGTAN BOMB

'WINGS' SHORT FILM SPECIAL – LIE (JIMIN SOLO DANCE)

This is Jimin's dance video for 'Lie', the track he co-wrote on the *Wings* album. It's simply shot and showcases his dancing skills perfectly as he delivers a controlled performance of elegance, passion and superb technical footwork. It's also an emotional piece which Jimin throws himself into with such energy that he needs a lie-down when he finishes, and judging from the BTL comments, he wasn't the only one!

him to sing and he warned fans that he would never be able to perform it live, but of course he did – beautifully. Similarly, on their *Bon Voyage* trip to Hawaii, when the boys look at the stars and make a wish, Jimin's wish was that he could sing. Jungkook's immediate reply was that he sings pretty well and Jin told him his singing is perfect. This, after all, is the guy who sang 'Serenpidity', who performed a wonderful duet with Jungkook on 'We Don't Talk Anymore' and whose smooth tones embellish so many BTS tracks.

Jimin's *selca* (selfie) obsession provides ARMY with a wealth of glorious photos. Recently, however, his *selca* love has developed into an interest in instant Polaroid pictures. He even listed looking at his Polaroid collection (he mounts and labels them in a book) of him and other band members as the number-one recreation on his happiness list.

ARMY have their own list of cherished Jimin moments, many of them gifs of him looking super-cute, smiling, looking shy, fiddling with his hair or revealing that mischievous grin. Such posts collect thousands of notes on Tumblr and it's not surprising that among many ARMY, Jimin is known as the group's recruiting fairy, because he attracts so many new fans.

Jimin's self-assumed role as the social media king of BTS has led to a great relationship with ARMY. In 2017, when he talked openly about his extreme dieting and how it caused him to collapse in dance practice, ARMY ensured that #JiminYouArePerfect was all over Twitter. Then in January 2018 they randomly got #ThankYouJimin trending worldwide on Twitter. It took Jimin completely by surprise, causing him to reply, 'What is this? hehe logged in because I wanted to leave something and saw this.'

Among the treasured videos for Jimin fans are the April 2017 'Eat Jin' episode where he sings along to 'Butterfly' as Jin plays guitar;

the *Run BTS!* karting episode where his punishment for coming last includes dancing to 'Blood, Sweat & Tears' while getting doused in water and then having to clean the floor; when he plays with Brandley the cat in the 2017 summer package; and the moment from *American Hustle Life*, when he leans into the camera to say 'Excuse me' in the most adorable accent (there's a YouTube video which repeats this five-second clip for five minutes!). As Jimin said himself on Korea's *After Show Club*, 'English is not a barrier when you are as cute as me!'

Who wouldn't love such a cute and playful young man? Certainly not the other BTS members, although they do endlessly tease him. Jimin even declared that 'being teased' was his

> 'English is not a barrier when you are as cute as me!'

speciality in the group. He's forever being reminded that he is the smallest of them all (although actually Suga runs him pretty close), that he has tiny hands (they are quite small) and that he constantly runs his hands through his hair (guilty as charged). But who do they all go to when they're feeling stressed? Jimin's ability to listen to others' troubles seems to be one of the key elements that makes BTS so strong.

Jungkook is often the teaser-in-chief. It's a strange role for the *maknae*, but perhaps he can get away with it because Jimin loves Jungkook like a little brother. Not that Jimin doesn't strike back. He often accuses Jungkook of copying him: being born in the same city, wearing the same earrings and having the same-colour contact lenses. They are often the ones seen messing about with each other and in November 2017 they took a trip together to Japan. You can see their holiday film on YouTube, shot and edited by Jungkook (so it's pretty much all Jimin!) and called *G.C.F in Tokyo*.

If Jungkook is his younger brother, then V is Jimin's twin. Together they make up the 95 line. They attended high school together, graduated together (check out the song '95 Graduation' they recorded as they couldn't make the ceremony) and continued to be best buddies as BTS went stratospheric. They are seen all over the Bangtan bombs, dancing, teasing other members and play-fighting. They send each other touching tweets, look out for each other when they've fallen on stage, and V even bought a thousand-dollar Gucci jumper for Jimin on his birthday. Their V-Live 'Mandaggo' shows, in theory about amusing regional differences between Jimin's Busan and V's Daegu dialects, show just how comfortable they are in each other's company.

At the end of their second *Bon Voyage* series, V reads his letter to Jimin. He recalls how they started at school together and have been friends ever since. He goes on to say, 'When I am in the bathroom crying, you cry with me. You also come to see me at dawn to laugh with me. You care about me and have me in your thoughts. You work hard for me and you understand me.' And then he sobs.

Since those trainee days, Jimin has transformed from being a cute boy to a handsome man. He's grown up in many ways and yet still maintains a youthful sense of fun and silliness. And, just as he has proved to be a great dancer and singer, he has also shown he is a caring and lovable friend to the group and to fans. He is indeed a vital piece of the BTS jigsaw – and as ARMY regularly like to point out, 'Once you Jimin, you can't Jimout!'

> He is a caring and lovable friend to the group and to fans.

THIRTEEN

RUNNING MEN

B TS could now call themselves not just idols but international stars who draw crowds of thousands to their concerts all around the world. Some fans at home might have been worried that success would change them. After all, this was a group who wrote songs from their own experiences as young people and who had built a unique relationship with ARMY through openness and communication. Would that suffer as they became more and more popular and their fan base expanded exponentially?

Not with these guys. One of the first things they did when they got back to Seoul was take a group of fans to the movies. Have you ever known a group to do that before? What's more, it was BTS keeping a promise they had made before they released 'I Need U'. Back then they had sworn that if they won a music show they would treat some fans to a night out with them at the movies (it was V's idea), and here they were, being true to their word.

The choice of movie was easy. After receiving good reviews for his solo mixtape and the 'P.D.D' collaboration with Warren G, RM was invited by Marvel to contribute to the soundtrack to their movie *Fantastic Four*. The result was 'Fantastic', which featured Mandy Ventrice, an American singer who had worked with Snoop Dogg,

Jay-Z and Kanye West. So, along with 200 fans, who were probably more interested in the occupants of the front row than the superhero movie, on 12 August the boys attended a special screening at the CGV Cinema in Wangsimni, Seoul, to support (and poke a little fun at!) their leader.

The fun and games couldn't last forever, though, and it wasn't long before the hard-working Bangtans were again on the plane to Japan. Back in June, BTS had achieved their first number-one single in Japan with a track written only in Japanese called 'For You'. The song has a soft, lyrical flow and a slow beat provided, somewhat unusually, by a plink-plonk piano and whistle. It's catchy and light, and the music video is a gem – worth catching if only to see Jungkook in a giant teddy bear outfit!

In contrast to the darkness of 'I Need U', the vibe here is warm and

BANGTAN BOMB

400-METER RELAY RACE @ ISAC

Having missed the Idol Star Athletics Championships in February 2015 because they were on tour in Japan, BTS eagerly return to the competition in August to defend their position as kings of the relay. With a team comprising Jimin, Jungkook, V and J-Hope, they had high expectations as they lined up against Seventeen, B1A4 and Teen Top. Have a look at this Bangtan bomb to see if they beat their K-pop rivals.

feel-good. In the smooth choreography sections the boys are dressed in black and white, but without the swag look, and the hip-hop moves are almost completely gone, too. They find solace in each other's company once more, but this time it's as a relief from the drudgery of their jobs: Suga is delivering pizzas, Jin is cleaning cars, V works in a convenience store, J-Hope waits on tables, Jimin is a washer-up, RM is still at the gas station and teddy bear Jungkook is handing out leaflets. Aww!

After wrapping up the Red Bullet tour to a rapturous reception in Hong Kong on 29 August, it was time for a very special occasion: Jungkook was going to be a Bangtan man! His eighteenth birthday fell on 1 September 2015 and, on the stroke of midnight, the other members surprised him with a strawberry birthday cake and promises of presents ranging from Timberlands (J-Hope) to a kiss (Jimin), while ARMY responded as only they can, getting #HappyJungkookDay trending worldwide on Twitter.

Little more than a month after leaving, BTS returned to North America in September to play some short sets in a Highlight Tour as part of their association with New York streetwear brand Community54. They went to San Francisco, Houston, Atlanta and, in a first trip to Canada, Toronto. Although they played 'N.O', 'Boy in Luv', 'Dope' and 'I Need U' with their customary energy and charisma, they had little onstage time to communicate with their audiences and poor organization of the events meant that unfortunately many fans didn't have a very positive experience.

As they continued to play festivals in Korea throughout the autumn, some intriguing teaser releases focused all eyes on the next comeback. The images for this were titled 'Je Ne Regrette Rien' (French for 'I regret nothing') and the feel was much lighter. Gone were the frowns and there was even a playfulness in some of the pictures. In fact, these concept photos were arguably the best yet. In the ones taken in a rural setting the boys seem very much at ease with themselves, while other pictures feature a more industrial scene and a punkier look, but even though pink-haired RM and mint-haired Suga pose and pout, the smiles escape nonetheless.

These concept photos were arguably the best yet.

Want to see something even more spectacular? Search for 'BTS on Stage: Prologue'. You should find a twelve-minute film posted by Big Hit. Don't worry about the language barrier, you just have to listen and watch and you'll be captivated. Released out of the blue at the beginning of October, it was an immediate hit with ARMY, who, of course, came up with their own theories about what's going on in the film.

As the film begins with a blood-splattered V cleaning himself up, is it safe to assume this is the aftermath of the 'I Need U' video, in which V became violent – perhaps killing his abusive father? Moving to another scenario, we see the boys hanging out and messing around, on one last, crazy road trip. There is a sense of wild abandon as they arm-wrestle and sword-fight, but there is also a forlorn undercurrent related to the music and the view through the lens of Jin's camcorder, especially as V plunges from a pier into the sea at the end.

Most theories assume that this is a ghost story. Big Hit posted, but later replaced, a version where, at the end of the credits, Jin is alone at the beach looking at the picture RM put in the glove compartment. Suga has disappeared in the photo. Could it be that, V aside, some or all of them died at the end of the music video? Is Jin trying to capture a time or emotion that has actually already passed?

Whatever the theory, the film set up the new album perfectly. The boys looked great, dressed down but bringing energy and charisma to every scene, the cinematography was spot on, and the previews of four of the tracks from the new mini-album provided a superb soundtrack.

On 29 November 2015, the nine-hundredth day since their debut, BTS played the last of a three-night stint at the Olympic Handball Gymnasium in Seoul. The 5,000-capacity venue was the largest they had played yet in Seoul but, of course, every night sold out instantly. They made use of the huge performing area, running around the T-shaped stage and even the aisles. They sang new arrangements of 'No More Dream' and 'N.O' and, less confined by strict choreography, they performed in a straight line, which enabled them to interact with their fans in a new way.

Of course, every night sold out instantly.

That this was a thank you to the home ARMY was made evident when they premiered their new songs not on a TV music show or an online video, but in front of those very fans. 'You guys are the first in the world to hear and see this performance,' was how Suga announced their new single, 'Run'. To a sea of chanting, light-stick wielding devotees, they then went on to sing, also for the first time, 'Never Mind', 'Butterfly' and 'Ma City'. If the audience reaction was anything to go by, the new mini-album was going to be a runaway success.

The *Korea Herald* reported that at the press conference for the concerts, RM had talked about the new songs, saying, 'No matter how old you are, you can slip and make mistakes, but I think society has become too harsh to judge those mistakes.' He went on to explain, 'We wanted to say that it's okay to fall down, to get hurt. All you have to do is get back up and keep running.' The 'never give up' message had already been seen in the album trailer. It featured simple, stylized outlines and bold colours featuring a boy, a basketball and hoop, and a butterfly with Suga at his most passionate and heartfelt yet, reflecting on

'We wanted to say that it's okay to fall down, to get hurt. All you have to do is get back up and keep running.'

his youth and delivering, in a raw shout, the key line: if you think you're going to crash, go faster.

The day after the final Handball Gymnasium concert saw the release of the music video for 'Run'. It amassed nearly 2 million YouTube views in the first twenty-four hours. A kind of sequel to 'I Need U', 'Run' was another collage of the boys having fun, partying, getting emotional and causing havoc. From V's backward fall into dark water at the start to Jimin being thrown fully clothed into a bath at the end, it was five minutes of high-octane action with bad boy BTS back vandalizing cars, spray-paint-tagging and fighting. It was not without wistful looks and meaningful stares, but the message about living your life, falling down and getting up again, came across strongly.

The Most Beautiful Moment in Life, Part 2 was released on 30 November 2015. Once again, it came in a choice of cover designs, this time peach or blue, and included a photobook featuring beautiful photos of the boys from both their nature and urban shoots. With this mini-album, BTS showed their mettle and proved the doubters wrong: not only had they continued to write their own top-quality songs, but the sophistication of both music and lyrics had improved, as had their attention to the smallest details in the production. More than one reviewer noted their bravery in pushing the boundaries of their musical style and continuing to produce amazing tracks.

More than one reviewer noted their bravery in pushing the boundaries of their musical style.

Suga's opening rap, 'Intro: Never Mind', which,

as was now customary, had been used as a trailer, lays out the mini-album's theme, and the next track 'Run' takes up the baton. Another step towards a full-on lush pop sound, 'Run' brings the rappers and the vocal line closer again. With a subtle instrumental dance backing, toned down rap and punchy chorus, it seems BTS have established a new style that combines passion and energy with a sentimental feel. As the practice choreography video for 'Run', released in early December, also showed, their dancing was maturing as well, because without the hip-hop posturing they could utilize their acting skills and be more expressive.

The next track, the artfully arranged 'Butterfly', features a soft synth backing track that allows the vocals, especially Jungkook's and V's, to spread smoothly and sweetly across the song like honey. More than this, though, it again shows how Suga's gift for lyrics is blossoming and the way he compares love to a fragile and elusive butterfly marks him out as a poet who is growing in stature.

The following track on the mini-album uses a different animal to communicate a concept. 'Whalien 52' is about the 52-hertz whale, a creature that calls at a unique frequency other whales cannot hear and has been described as the loneliest whale in the world. The tune is lilting and hypnotic and, although the metaphor is not as subtle as 'Butterfly', Bangtan turn it into an empathetic exploration of feeling alone, which is just as effective.

Next it's all aboard for the train to 'Ma City'. A live favourite, this is a non-stop express ride with a driving beat and a retro, almost disco, feel. As the group members eulogize about their home towns (with Suga admitting he brags about Daegu on every album), it's a reminder that, unlike most K-pop groups, BTS are free to use their dialects and are not ashamed of where they come from.

Don't ignore the track '뱁새' that follows just because there is no direct English translation. It's sometimes known as 'Silver Spoon' but often called 'Try Hard' or 'Baepsae', which translates as 'Crow-Tit', a small Korean bird. According to a Korean saying, if a crow-tit walks like the long-legged stork, it will damage its legs, and BTS portray their generation as the crow-tits expected to walk like their stork parents, even though expectations have changed. Set to a South-East-Asian-sounding beat, it is one of BTS's angriest songs yet, as RM almost spits out how, thanks to those who came before them, his generation has suffered.

The skit features a light-hearted chat about how far they have come, before two final tracks, some say the best of the album. 'Autumn Leaves' (sometimes known as 'Dead Leaves' or 'Fallen Leaves') gives us another metaphor as the season changes and leaves hanging on to branches mirror a love growing cold and hanging on desperately. With an even line distribution, the song highlights the vocal talents of every single member.

The high production standards are maintained right through to the outro, a song titled 'House of Cards', which compares a fragile love affair to a structure precariously built from playing cards. To a dreamy string backing track, voices weave in and out in the smoothest of transitions as we pick out V's falsetto, Jin's pleas, Jimin's raspy tone and Jungkook's alluring, almost cracked voice.

BTS had treated the Seoul ARMY to the first live performance of 'Run', but the comeback stage was pretty special, too. At the 2015 MAMAs in early December, although the *daesang* grand prize escaped them again (BIGBANG and EXO took the honours), BTS picked up a special award as best worldwide performer – one of the first signs that their global popularity could mean they would eclipse other groups.

For those who enjoyed the previous year's Block B collaboration, this time they took on GOT7 in a special stage. The performance of 'Virtual Boys' began with a rap battle between RM and GOT7's Jackson, then a dance-off with J-Hope and Yugyeom, before both groups, BTS in white and GOT7 in black, united in a superbly synchronized display. The video of the joint group owning the MAMA stage is still cherished by ARMY, perhaps because of all K-pop groups, GOT7 seem closest to BTS. Then, as BTS followed with their own comeback stage, they again brought the audience to their feet. MAMA was becoming a pretty special event for the boys.

Once they had persuaded J-Hope to say the single would flop, there really was no doubt it was going to be a hit. The video secured wins on music awards programmes *Show Champion* and *The Show Choice* while the boys were busy in Japan, although they were back in time to perform on *Music Bank* and see their track win again, despite

BANGTAN BOMB

'RUN' CHRISTMAS VERSION

Suga in a santa cap ... Jimin in antlers ... Jin in pink ear muffs ... This isn't 'Run' as we know it. There's no enigmatic storyline, no heavy make-up, no sensational choreography, but instead there are a lot of laughs and we're treated to Jungkook sleeping sweetly and Suga definitely not running. If you're in need of Christmas cheer, this is the bomb for you.

fierce competition from Psy. Three wins in a week! And to think that just a year ago they were desperate for even a solitary victory. They had come a long way.

'Run' reached number eight in the Korean singles charts, while *The Most Beautiful Moment in Life, Part 2* matched *Part 1* by topping the album charts. However, it was the splash they made stateside that was most remarkable. Over there, the mini-album topped the Billboard Heatseekers and World Albums charts for four weeks, a record for a South Korean act. And they weren't finished there; when the Billboard 200 came out in the week before Christmas, BTS was at 171! Although ten K-pop acts had already matched that position, BTS were the first to achieve it without being a Big Three group.

BANGTAN BOMB

IT'S THE POSE WHEN BTS SLEEP NORMALLY

If you've watched any BTS interviews you'll know by now that BTS's favourite thing (after ARMY, obviously) is sleeping. So here's a Bangtan bomb from their time in Chile about sleeping, or trying to sleep, or waking, or walking on your hands (J-Hope is one excellent hand walker!). Whatever. It's Jimin on camera and more super-charming goofing around from J-Hope, Jungkook and Suga.

In Japan, BTS had followed their June 2015 number-one hit 'For You' with a Japanese version of 'I Need U', which reached number two in December. That month, 25,000 fans had attended two sold-out concerts in Yokohama, Japan's second-largest city. Meanwhile, out in the USA, *The Most Beautiful Moment in Life, Part 2*, spent a total of sixteen weeks on Billboard's World Albums Chart. Even Europe was catching on to BTS as they took Best Korean Act at the 2015 MTV Europe Music Awards.

At home a victory on *Music Bank* at the end of the promotion on 8 January 2016 marked their fifth triumph of the comeback and their tenth to date. The awards season over, the Christmas period had also proved fruitful as they picked up *bonsangs* at the Golden Disc Awards and the Seoul Music Awards. That yearned-for *daesang* was tantalizingly close but still eluded them.

FACT FILE

Name: Kim Taehyung
Nicknames: V, Taetae, Human Gucci, Vante
Date of birth: 30 December 1995
Birthplace: Daegu, South Korea
Height: 1.79 metres (5'10")
Education: Changnam Elementary School,
Geochang Middle School, Daegu First High
School, Korean Arts High School,
Global Cyber University
Chinese zodiac: Pig
Star sign: Capricorn

FOURTEEN

KIM TAEHYUNG/V: PRINCE OF DUALITY

They are both devilishly good-looking, stylish and love to sing. But there the similarity between Kim Taehyung and BTS's singer and dancer, V, ends. Yes, they might be one and the same 95-line boy from Daegu, but Taehyung's persona changes radically when he goes out on that stage. Watch any BTS performance and you'll see V being cool, sophisticated and professional; watch a Bangtan bomb or an offstage video and you'll often discover the lovably dorkish Taetae, messing about, being plain silly or lost in a world of his own.

In November 2016, during the encore of a BTS concert in the Gocheok Sky Dome in Korea, it was V who came to the front of the stage to address the 17,000 fans. In a heartbreaking speech, he explained that recently, when the group was in the Philippines, he had received news that his grandmother had died. Fans and group members shed tears with him as he told of his love for her and how he had planned to send her a special message when the group were on television, but now would never get the chance.

Taehyung had been particularly close to his paternal grandmother.

She had brought him up for fourteen years as his parents, traditional Korean farmers, were busy working. He was a boy who loved to play outside, but paid attention to his studies too. Then, as he went to middle school, still not quite a teenager, he began to dream. He wanted to be a singer.

As he went to middle school, still not quite a teenager, he began to dream. He wanted to be a singer.

Taking his father's advice to learn an instrument, Taehyung took up the saxophone. He worked at it and became a competent player, winning first prize in a regional competition. With his eye already on becoming an idol, he joined a dance club and soon gave up the sax to spend more time on the dance floor.

He had joined a dance academy, but a few months after starting high school in Daegu in 2011, his life changed – dramatically. When Big Hit held auditions in Daegu, Taehyung had no intention of trying out, but went along with a friend. There, the good-looking young lad was spotted by one of the Big Hit staff. She encouraged him to audition, but Taehyung declined as he didn't have his parents' consent. Sensing the boy might have something, she called his parents, got permission and he was quickly on stage, dancing, rapping and even telling jokes. He didn't believe he had a chance, but Big Hit contacted him and told him he had passed – the only one from that audition who had.

So Taehyung moved into the Big Hit dorm and, wearing the padded red jacket his mother had sent him so he stood out, enrolled in high school in Seoul (where he was joined by Jimin). Trainee days don't seem to have scarred Taehyung as much as the others. He liked school, loved the dance lessons and although he admits to missing his family, he was having fun with his new friends at school and in the company. He seems to have been happy living in the present, taking his place in BTS in his stride and not wondering when they would debut. Although it was hard work and intense, Taehyung was living his dream and was determined to enjoy it.

Finally debut did appear on the horizon and Taehyung chose a name. He rejected Six and Lex and went with V for victory, but he was in for a shock. Big Hit had decided his membership of BTS would be kept secret until just before debut. His identity would be hidden, no photos of him would be released and he couldn't record vlogs like the others. He went to RM and Jungkook's graduations, his back had appeared in Jimin's selfie (everyone had assumed it was Jungkook) and Jimin had even taken his school uniform (while V was sleeping!) to wear in the 'Graduation Song' video. Poor V would sometimes sit by himself and pretend to do a vlog and, as if that wasn't sad enough, as they were recording their final pre-debut group vlog, V was actually in the room, standing in the corner keeping out of shot!

However, once he was revealed, V was an immediate hit with fans. They liked the handsome figure who flicked off his glasses during the 'No More Dream' performance, although they noted that offstage he could be a little, well, strange. He'd sometimes speak a made-up language, have an incredibly blank expression, wave his hands or make off-the-wall comments like saying his chosen superpower would be to be able to talk to cars. It was charming and K-pop fans have a word for it: 4D.

There is a K-pop tradition of describing artists as

> Although it was hard work and intense, Taehyung was living his dream and was determined to enjoy it.

> His chosen superpower would be to be able to talk to cars.

'4D' and it's a flattering term, meaning they are quirky and different, and have added personality and charisma. Suga later said he originally thought Taehyung was acting, that people like that didn't exist, but came to realize his unique behaviour was authentic, and ARMY affectionately began calling him '4D', 'Alien' or 'Blank Tae'. However, even as early as summer 2015, Taehyung let it be known that he didn't really like those names and most fans respectfully stopped.

Nevertheless, he has remained the most unconventional member of the group and in a 2015 interview with Korean magazine *The Star*, Taehyung said, 'I am not scared of looking ugly and I'm thankful that [my fans] like me even when I pull weird faces. I don't plan on looking handsome in an unnatural way. That would be a burden.'

It certainly seems to work. Taetae (a name he seems happy with) has a great relationship with ARMY. He has become a star at fan meets through the unique way he interacts with people. In 2017 he told a girl that if she gets unwanted attention from boys she could tell them she was dating Taehyung! However, when he pulled a girl's hair to get her to look at him, only a message from the girl herself, revealing she was an old friend and that Taehyung was messing around, calmed down a raging online debate about his behaviour.

Taehyung ... doesn't follow the crowd, but always manages to look stylish, whatever he wears.

This is the guy who came up with the 'I purple you' phrase, explaining in a tweet that as purple is the last colour in the rainbow it means 'I will love you forever'. And who couldn't love him? Many ARMY clearly do. In December 2017 his fan club, V Baidu, ran a whole week of messages in Times Square, New York, to celebrate his birthday.

Taehyung's out-there persona extends to his

fashion sense. He doesn't follow the crowd, but always manages to look stylish, whatever he wears. Back in the days when they were rookies, he would take scissors to his shirts and jeans (Jungkook claims he taught him to do this). He even asked on Twitter for suggestions on where to make the holes. He has since developed a quirky but chic look by combining various styles that might include any combination of round glasses, roll-neck jumpers, French-style striped long-sleeved shirts and oversize coats. However, in recent times tigers and snakes have been a constant theme because V just loves the brand Gucci; not only the clothes but the shades, rings, neck bows and watches. No wonder the man who hates nicknames earned himself another: Human Gucci.

Like all the members, Taehyung has given ARMY many moments to cherish. *American Hustle Life* provided memes of the classic 'Beach! Bitch?' misunderstanding with Jimin, as well as his misjudged attempt to impress Coolio with his enthusiastic 'Turn Up!' exclamation. A much-loved TV episode of *Star King* (the clip is on YouTube) saw him pull off some serious dance moves while wearing twelve-centimetre (about four-and-a-half-inch) heels. Various videos show how soft Taetae gets when kids and babies are in the vicinity and ARMY just love his Dubsmash app lip-syncing.

His tweets also reveal V's love of art, from the Van Gogh *Starry Night* picture hanging on his wall in the dorm to the visit he and RM made to the Art Institute of Chicago. He is also a big fan of Australian photographer Ante Badzim, whose simple but beautiful photos inspired V to take his own pictures. He uploaded some of them with the hashtag #Vante (another nickname!) and came to the attention of the photographer himself, who dedicated a photo to V in return.

The other group members all love Taetae too, even if Jin complains he is a little noisy and Suga says he sometimes just doesn't get him. A love of gaming and a light-hearted approach to life has led him to bond with ace gamer and super-*maknae*, Jungkook, but Taehyung and Jimin possibly have the closest friendship in the whole group, and V's heartfelt letter to his friend on the *Bon Voyage 2* boat revealed just how grateful Taetae is for his fellow 95-liner's care and affection.

That letter was quite timely. Jimin seemed to be a tiny bit jealous when Taehyung became close to some of his actor friends and complained that Taetae was always telling his actor friends he loved them, but never the members. Taehyung replied that it was because BTS felt like family and they didn't need telling. Besides, Taehyung is a real social butterfly. He has so many friends outside BTS and is regularly pictured with celebrities and idols. He seems to be able to make friends anywhere, having befriended BTOB's Sungjae, singer Jang Moon Bok and Block B's Park Kyung during rest breaks.

V has so many friends outside BTS and is regularly pictured with celebrities and idols.

In December 2017, we were introduced to Taetae's latest friend. Jin was conducting a live stream for his birthday when V appeared at the window holding the cutest puppy imaginable. We soon found out that this was his new dog, a Pomeranian that he named Yeontan (which translates as 'charcoal briquette'). Because of BTS's busy schedule, Yeontan left the dorm to stay with Taehyung's parents, but they still see each other regularly. In the 2018 *festa* interview, Taehyung revealed how the puppy now follows him around but runs away when he tries to catch him – and that 'Tan' had gained too much puppy fat!

As ARMY got to know Taehyung, so they became accustomed to V. It surprised many to hear those deep, soulful notes coming from someone so adept at *aygeo* cute faces, but V's rich tone adds contrast to the higher register of the other vocalists, although he can take it up the scale with ease, too. There are so many examples of his singing talent, but his solo tracks 'Stigma' and 'Singularity', his collaboration with RM, '4 O'Clock', or his cover of Adele's 'Someone Like You' are exquisite.

V's stage presence is also pretty awesome. He feels the emotion of every word he sings and he works the crowd with a perfectly placed, but not overused, wink, smile or subtle lick of the lips. His dancing is sharp and confident, and he has created a moment audiences anticipate with great excitement in 'Boyz with Fun', where the other members (and sometimes backing dancers) have to copy his improvised choreography.

BANGTAN BOMB

V'S DREAM CAME TRUE – 'HIS CYPHER PT. 3 SOLO STAGE'

When J-Hope took the third place in BTS's rap line, V's status as vocalist in the group was confirmed, but he remained a frustrated rapper. He raps in the practice room and at fan meets, and sometimes seems to bristle with jealousy during the cyphers. He has admitted he wanted to switch bodies with Suga for 'Cypher Pt. 3', so imagine his glee when he was given the solo part in the 2016 *festa* performance. This bomb shows not only his memorable rap, but also how the other members help him prepare for his big moment.

In 2016, V temporarily got himself another name: Han Sung. He was cast in a historical drama television series called *Hwarang: The Poet Warrior Youth*, which focused on the lives and loves of a group of young men in Korea over two thousand years ago. Taehyung's portrayal of a lovable and innocent character, the youngest of the group, was appreciated by audiences (and not just ARMY), especially in the scenes of high emotion, and his fellow actors commented on his natural talent and his work ethic.

Thank heaven that Big Hit member of staff was so determined to get his parents' approval for the original audition. Taehyung brings so much more to BTS than his vocals and dance skills; he provides a vibrant personality, a unique and stylish visual sense, and multiple performance talents that can only help the group move forward. V and Taehyung: let's celebrate the duality!

FIFTEEN

BTS ON FIRE!

I n late 2015, just before the release of *The Most Beautiful Moment in Life, Part 2*, the sports brand Puma announced an endorsement deal with BTS. Brand endorsement is a major part of K-pop and the fact that a multinational company as massive as Puma chose to sign up the Bangtan Boys tells us a lot about how far they had come since their debut. Even if their initial advert, which featured them wearing Puma and dancing in the street to a rewritten version of 'Run', was a little cheesy!

Cheesy was something BTS might have to get used to as major idols. Early in 2016 they were invited to appear with top girl group G-Friend in a song for Family Love Day, a campaign encouraging families to spend at least one day a week together. On YouTube the song's title is translated as 'Family Song' and, well, it may not be BTS's finest three and a half minutes (you get the sense Suga doesn't really want to be there!), but they all look cute in their smart school uniforms and, if you're looking for a straightforward BTS dance to learn, this is a good place to start. The 'making of' video also has some particularly cute pics of the guys as young children.

In February, BTS returned to the Idol Star Athletics in a team called Beat to the End with their friends GOT7 and girl groups Twice and Bestie. They retained their relay kings title, with J-Hope, Jimin, Jungkook and V taking gold in the 4 × 100 metres and then took part in the eight-team *ssireum* tournament. This traditional Korean form of wrestling involves each competitor wearing a loose belt which is gripped by his opponent, who attempts to bring him down. A team of V, Jungkook and Jin saw off BTOB and Teen Top to meet VIXX in the final. Jungkook won the first bout, but V couldn't wrap the tournament up so it was all down to Jin, who met singer Ken in the final bout. Although there were a lot of smiles, it was tense as the two faced off. They moved around the ring holding each other like ballroom dancers before Ken, sensing his moment, forced the slightly off-balance Jin to the floor. Never mind, he still looked good!

No one actually died as a result of Big Hit posting comeback

BANGTAN BOMB

BTS'S RHYTHMICAL FARCE! LOL

This bomb is a big favourite of ARMY all around the world. In a backstage area, various combinations of Bangtan Boys pretend to meet each other. Their reactions are exaggerated and usually accompanied by a scream of 'Yahhhh'. What are they doing? Working out a new form of greeting? Some form of improvised drama? Or perhaps it's just inspired messing around? Whatever. It's ninety seconds of nonsense that you'll watch again and again.

concept photos for their compilation album in April 2016. But given ARMY's online reaction to the new blond Jin, you'd be forgiven for thinking someone had. With a wavy, back-combed look, Jin wrecked biases in seconds as he posed in the photoshoot. Not that he was the only one to change his hair colour; Suga kept the grey but all the others had been at the dye. RM had gone for blue-grey, Jimin was back to black, V's hair had taken on a pinky-orange hue, Jungkook's messy locks were dark brown and J-Hope sported a layered, light brown style.

For the day and night sets of concept photos for *The Most Beautiful Moment in Life: Young Forever*, they posed in a clearing on Jeju Island, an island off the Korean peninsula. They were on an adventure involving a campervan and a hot-air balloon, and the location choice allowed the boys' bright colours to contrast against a washed-out landscape and a big sky, with a Polaroid format adding an extra effect on the night photos.

The shoot presented a change of style for the Bangtan crew. Gone was the punked-up look we saw in *Part Two* and in its place was finery – and shorts! The clothes were dominated by Gucci, with frilly shirts, ribbons, neck clasps and berets, but there were also smart, tight-fitting, two-button suits, V carrying off a powder-blue version with particular aplomb. It was the sophistication of a bygone era combined with camp, humour and a carefree attitude. Most ARMY barely seemed to notice, though. They were still getting over Suga's freckles, the return of Jimin's dimples and – wow – Jin's hair!

Young Forever, BTS's April 2016 release, was a twenty-three-track compilation album featuring the songs from both *The Most Beautiful Moment in Life* albums, with six remixes and full versions of the previous two albums' outros as well as three new tracks. However, the fact that it was a compilation didn't stop Big Hit giving it the full build-up with teasers and previews.

They also trailed and announced BTS's first solo concerts of 2016, BTS Live The Most Beautiful Moment in Life On Stage: Epilogue, to be held at the Olympic Gymnastics Arena in South Korea where, once again, ARMY would be the first to witness the new choreography live. Their first ever concerts at the 15,000-capacity venue played only by K-pop giants sold out instantly. The trailer for the shows featured the smartly suited band members facing the flashing lights of the paparazzi as they trod the red carpet. It was an experience they were going to have to get used to in real life.

Each of the three new tracks on *Young Forever* were released with their own music videos, beginning with 'Epilogue: Young Forever'. The video showed flashbacks to 'I Need You' and 'Run', along with images of individual members trapped in, and eventually breaking free from, a wire fence maze. The song builds from a softly spoken statement about living in the now, enjoying the moment but not being scared to move on, to the unashamed optimism of the anthemic chorus, an almost irresistible singalong that dominates the final section.

In the first week of May, BTS dropped the music video for 'Fire'. Basically a dance video set in a now almost familiar derelict warehouse, it was further enlivened by Suga remotely exploding a dark figure, uncontrollable flames, a falling car slamming to the ground and some great acting. Junkook's wide-eyed look, V's video game-playing and even Jimin's 'Ow!' were highlights that demonstrated a new level of confidence in front of the camera. The video hit 1 million views in just six hours and in just

The video hit 1 million views in just six hours.

over two days had amassed 10 million views. It was the best reaction yet.

'Fire' is a rocking, beat-thumping number that charges out of the starting blocks and incorporates all those elements that make their high-tempo tracks so exciting. A rap intro – check (good job, J-Hope); a singalong chorus – check; an infectious la-la-la – check; a cheeky insert – check; a false stop and a renewed start – check. The lyrics pick up the themes from the whole trilogy. They ask their listeners to run with them, not to be afraid to live, to embrace the fire and burn everything up – with passion, desire, risk and ambition.

The accompanying dance was also suitably fearless. In interviews, the group said how difficult it was to master Keone Madrid's choreography, but they completely nailed it. A feast of energy and movement sees them switching effortlessly from speedy, almost martial arts-style whipping movements to slo-mo moves, interspersed with moments of cheekiness (dabs!) and *aegyo*. And they never let up on the perfect synchronicity. On top of all this, you just have to admire their stamina: watch the dance practice video on YouTube to catch the full intensity of the performance.

The third of the new releases, the more emotional 'Save Me', followed within a few weeks and had the vocal line to the fore. A more conventional BTS lover's plea, it nevertheless grabs the attention with a superb synth beat of muted whistles and xylophones.

The music video was a one-shot take of the group dancing on barren sand dunes. It was the first time they had danced to the choreography of Norwegian-based team The Quick Style, who brought in some subtlety and contemporary dance moves while taking nothing away from the customary razor-sharp group dance. And, of course, BTS left us with a tease. As the video fades to black, a message is typed on screen. It reads 'BOY MEETS'. We wait for the next word, but that's it.

This trio of tracks would consolidate BTS's status as one of the top groups in Korea.

Only BTS could leave fans wondering like that!

It was soon apparent that this trio of tracks would consolidate BTS's status as one of the top groups in Korea. On the day of its release, 'Fire' achieved the group's first chart 'all-kill', topping all the major real-time charts simultaneously, and BTS's performances of the song on *M Countdown*, *Music Bank* and *Inkigayo* brought them three more music-show trophies. Additionally, *Young Forever* went on to top the Korean album chart and stayed there for two consecutive weeks.

In the USA, the BTS ripple gained momentum. *Young Forever* became their second consecutive album to make the Billboard 200, reaching as high as 106, while on the World Digital Songs chart they set a record never before achieved by a K-pop group: with 'Fire', 'Save Me' and 'Epilogue: Young Forever' they had three tracks in the chart at the same time.

In June 2016, Big Hit had something new planned for BTS on V-Live. A preview episode of *Bon Voyage* showed the boys in the company boardroom discussing where they would like to go (Hawaii or rural South Korea) and who they would like to go with (J-Hope or Jimin). All this seems forgotten when they arrive back at the dorm – yes, we get to see the dorm at last! – to discover they're going to northern Europe and they're all going together. And so begins the V-Live pay-per-view series *Bon Voyage*: eight forty-minute episodes (with extra 'behind camera' videos also available) following their ten-day backpacking trip across Norway, Sweden and Finland.

For boys who have spent at least four years doing little else but practising, performing and recording, this was a chance to have a holiday courtesy of Hitman Bang, but when they tour, everything is arranged for them by the company. Right from the start it is beautifully chaotic as panic and indecision reign in the dorm as they try to decide which clothes to pack. Suga is methodical as he counts his pairs of clean socks, Jungkook plays the *maknae*, asking everyone else what they are taking, and Jimin just can't make up his mind what to pack.

> Right from the start it is beautifully chaotic as panic and indecision reign in the dorm as they try to decide which clothes to pack.

Their first stop is Bergen in Norway. Thanks to RM's fluent English they negotiate their way from the airport to the city, only to discover Jimin has left his bag on the airport bus. It's surprising that the series wasn't called *The Lost Boys* because when they're not actually lost themselves they seem to be forever losing things – bags, iPads, tickets. When RM loses his passport, it is no longer funny; to the shock of the other members, he is forced to abandon the trip.

As their journey takes them on to Sweden and Finland, we see the others enjoying their time together as they sail down fjords, go on a bike ride, stay in an RV campervan, experience a sauna and cold lake dip, and visit Santa Park. This is BTS as normal guys in their twenties travelling together. They can't believe it, it's so relaxing, and J-Hope even discovers a phrase to keep the few fans they do encounter at bay: 'Sorry – important business!'

> The trip ... made them value each other's company even more and appreciate what they have achieved.

On their last evening, as they sit by the lakeside reading the handwritten letters sent by Bang Si-hyuk and their manager Sejin to mark their forthcoming third anniversary, it does seem like the trip has made them value each other's company even more and appreciate what they have achieved. As Suga says in his closing comments, they are all like family now.

In the summer, BTS flew out to Europe to top the bill at KCON in Paris and then to the States to the Newark and Los Angeles conventions. As Jeff Benjamin wrote in *Billboard*, 'If their headliner status didn't already indicate it, perhaps the charts can confirm that a new boy band is in town and ready to take over.' With the new tracks from *Young Forever*, plus 'Dope', 'I Need U' and 'Boyz with Fun', BTS now had a set full of sure-fire crowd-pleasers.

According to the organizers of the Newark KCON, which took place on 24 and 25 June, the 18,000-ticket BTS concert sold out faster than Bruce Springsteen. RM shared the MC duties on day one of the convention and the group closed the event on the second day. ARMY were reportedly the loudest fans ever heard at the venue and BTS even had the confidence to insert their own favourite, 'Cypher Pt. 3: Killer' from *Dark & Wild* into the set. That went down a storm, too.

The next month they repeated the feat at the West Coast edition of KCON, which ran from 29 to 31 July. In the *LA Times*, August Brown wrote, 'BTS closed out the night with a reminder of why the group is one of K-pop's most lasting and influential acts ... The group bounded over the KCON stage with precision and verve, and took long, live turns to show off the members' rhyming dexterity in the thick of it all. K-pop has everything now, and Sunday's finale showed just how good a lot of it can be.'

In between the French and the two US KCON concerts came the great tradition known as *festa*, BTS and ARMY's annual celebration of their debut, now three years in the memory. It got off to a flying start with a free download of a new track, 'I Know', a tender duet recorded by RM and Jungkook, before the fun kicked in with a specially choreographed version of favourite song 'Baepsae' and the family photo albums. These included some poses of the boys in their black tie and blazers or in uniforms complete with peaked caps, as well as Jin in a chef's outfit and a hilarious set of Suga and J-Hope goofing around in their orange 'SOPE' tracksuits (a video of the photoshoot is now on YouTube).

The next video specially uploaded for *festa* stunned even dedicated ARMY. Titled 'J-Hope Dance Practice for 2015 Begins Concert', it was a sixty-second clip of J-Hope absolutely tearing up the dancefloor at Big Hit's studio and suddenly it was clear quite what the guy was capable of and how much he was holding back in the group dances – even in their most electric choreographies.

The summer ended as it had begun with BTS selling out huge venues in Japan for the last of their 2016 BTS Live The Most Beautiful Moment in Life On Stage: Epilogue concerts and competing in the second of the year's Idol Star Athletics. Here they once again took the 4 × 100 metres relay (would they ever be defeated?) as J-Hope, Jimin, Jungkook and Suga beat teams from BTOB and B.A.P, but they proved less successful in an archery competition. A Bangtan bomb shows them looking good in their team tracksuit tops and shorts, Jimin now with blond hair, but they didn't really seem to be taking it seriously enough to win.

Young Forever – especially the three new songs – had taken BTS up yet another level. Somehow, these small company guys, writing much of their own music, were winning over not only their home country, but also their South-East Asian neighbours, as well as gaining thousands of fans in the Middle East, Australasia, South America, Europe and, whisper it quietly, they even had a foothold in the USA.

JUNGKOOK

FACT FILE

Name: Jeon Jungkook
Nicknames: Jungkook, Jungkookie, Kookie, JK, Nochu, Seagull, Golden *Maknae*, Bunny
Date of birth: 1 September 1997
Birthplace: Busan, South Korea
Height: 1.78 metres (5'10")
Education: Baekyang Middle School, Shingu Middle School, School of Performance Arts High School
Chinese zodiac: Ox
Star sign: Virgo

SIXTEEN

JEON JUNGKOOK:
THE GOLDEN MAKNAE

I t was RM who came up with the name 'Golden *Maknae*' for Jungkook, although chances are ARMY would have come up with it themselves before too long, for the baby of BTS is multi-talented, not just as a singer, dancer and gorgeous-looking band member, but also at practically anything else he turns his hand to. Barely a teenager when he started his journey to stardom, this baby has shown such maturity in coping with the adversity faced by the group and the stresses of idol life.

Having a special *maknae* is common in K-pop groups. The word refers to the youngest member and they are often the cutest and most playful, and receive the most affection from the others in the group. All this is true of Jungkook – just see how BTS looked out for him in rookie stage performances or protected him during group interviews and TV shows in their early days. However, it soon became apparent that this *maknae* had something else, a real natural-born talent, and as BTS developed and grew in confidence, so did Jungkook. Those who followed the group from debut had to take a breath and ask themselves just when he changed from being the cherished child to the jewel of the family.

Like Jimin, Jungkook grew up in the city of Busan. He lived with his mother, father and older brother, Jeon Junghun, so he had some experience of being the baby of the family. Indeed, his brother has shared many adorable pictures of his infant sibling online. It's probably fair to say that Jungkook didn't excel at school, except in physical education, art and music, and in elementary school sport was particularly important to him. He took taekwondo lessons, eventually earning a black belt, played soccer and showed a particular aptitude for badminton. He used to dream of growing up to be a professional badminton player, and when his parents bought him his first computer his first games were e-sports.

> He used to dream of growing up to be a professional badminton player.

Jungkook discovered music in middle school, especially the songs of the King of K-pop, G-Dragon, as the BIGBANG vocalist's solo career went stratospheric with 'Heartbreaker'. The seventh grader began singing and was even inspired to try street dance, joining a local b-boy club. By 2011, he felt confident enough to audition for *Superstar K*, the biggest TV talent show in South Korea (think *The X-Factor* or *American Idol*).

After queuing for hours along with thousands of other hopefuls at the Busan auditions, Jungkook was given his two-minute opportunity. With a slightly shapeless haircut and wearing a long-sleeved white T-shirt, he looked very sweet as he sang 2AM's 'This Song' and IU's 'Lost Child' (Jungkook fans can find the performance online). His voice was breaking at the time and he says that was why he didn't progress beyond the qualifying round and make it on to TV, but he clearly had something, because following the audition he was contacted by no fewer than seven agencies who had seen his performance, including JYP, one of the Big Three.

What made him choose Big Hit? He saw RM in full rap mode and decided there and then. 'I thought RM was so cool, so I wanted to sign with them,' he told the *New Yang Nam Show* in 2017. Like the other trainees, he arrived alone in Seoul and took his place in the dorm. He was only thirteen years old, but he had to change schools, find his way around a new city, meet new friends and begin training to be an idol with much older trainees.

> He was contacted by no fewer than seven agencies who had seen his performance.

Jungkook has admitted that the loud, sometimes boisterous schoolboy from Busan immediately became a quiet and shy trainee in Seoul. Members have recalled how he would wait until everyone was asleep before he took a shower and that he would avoid singing in front of them and cry if they pressed him. When Bang Si-hyuk told him there was no emotion in his dancing, it must have taken all of Kookie's strength not to pack up and go home.

Instead, the young teenager who had never been on a plane before went to America. Big Hit had booked him into an intense street-dance course at the famous dance academy Movement Lifestyle in LA. He found it tough, but learned a lot in just a month and still managed to buy a skateboard and master another new skill. By the end of 2012, Jungkook had been revealed as the sixth and apparently final (not including the hidden V) member of BTS. The stage name Seagull, which is the official bird of the city of Busan and the nickname of its baseball team, was suggested, but Jungkook chose to stick with his own name.

Jungkook's shyness was still an issue. Bang Si-hyuk admitted it was a gamble allowing him to debut, as many at Big Hit believed he wasn't ready, but BTS team spirit kicked in. It must be remembered that he was still only fifteen. Kookie has often spoken about how Jin looked after him, cooking for him and driving him to school, and Suga gave him fatherly advice such as his appalled reaction in *American Hustle Life* when Jungkook looks forward to being able to get a tattoo. And their faith wasn't misplaced. As he grew in confidence, Jungkook began to deliver. From 'Graduation Song', posted in February 2013 shortly after he had graduated from middle school, fans became aware of the *maknae's* sweet voice, and after the debut they realized he was a sharp dancer as well. He still wasn't a live wire in interviews, but that could be overlooked for now.

As Jungkook progressed through high school, he became a central figure in the group.

As Jungkook progressed through high school, he became a central figure in the group. He would now feature prominently in choreographies and his smooth, sometimes husky, vocals could be heard more and more in BTS tracks. Eventually, on *Wings*, Jungkook would get his own song, 'Begin', written by RM, but with his personal input. He said he felt embarrassed to explain the lyrics to the other members as it tells of how he cried for them when their workload had become too much, but they are heartfelt sentiments and he sings it beautifully. Then, before *Love Yourself: Tear* was released, Jungkook took the vocals for the trailer, 'Euphoria', a track many ARMY were disappointed not to find on the album.

Over the intervening years, Jungkook would post a collection of impressive cover songs – many of them in English. A self-proclaimed Belieber, he has recorded, to many fans' delight, Justin Bieber's 'Boyfriend', 'Nothing Like Us', 'Purpose' and '2U', but also Tori Kelly's 'Paper Hearts', Adam Levine's 'Lost Stars', Charlie Puth's 'We Don't

Talk Anymore' (to which Puth tweeted 'Love this Jungcook') and enough others for YouTubers to create an imaginary covers album. In February 2018, he tweeted a cover of Park Won's 'All of My Life', where he played piano and sang stripped-down vocals. Within days it had over a million likes.

As Jungkook's engaging and playful personality emerged in BTS video and TV appearances, he was invited to guest on various variety shows. In 2016 he appeared in *King of Mask Singer*, a TV series which pitches K-pop singers against each other while disguising their real identities. Jungkook featured as Fencing Man, wearing a spectacular silver mask. Although he didn't win, his cover of BIGBANG's 'If You' is a song ARMY still treasure.

He would also feature in a series called *Celebrity Bromance*. Jungkook was paired with Minwoo, a thirty-six-year-old first-generation K-pop star from the group Shinhwa. The older star's caring nature did much

BANGTAN BOMB

JUST WATCHING JUNGKOOK LIP SYNC SHOW

If you think Jungkook is all about soulful sweet harmonies, just watch him rock out with V to Linkin Park's 'Given Up'. To an amused audience of Jimin and J-Hope, he gets the air guitar out and lip-syncs (including expletives) as if he was a fluent English speaking, nu-metal guitar hero. Even as a rock dude, he still looks pretty cute!

to help bring Jungkook out of his shell and the scenes where they meet amid puppies in the dog café or when Jungkook goes rock climbing to earn dinner are worth watching. Less successful was his appearance on *Flower Crew*, a travel-reality series. There was some controversy as some of the other participants were seen as being rude to Jungkook and the voting process on which the show relied was skewed due to Kookie's popularity. He was even seen to mouth 'Don't vote for me' in embarrassment.

Meanwhile, his dorm mates had discovered their *maknae* had many other skills. The competitive youngster would invariably win the games they played, his drawing skills were more than impressive (it's genetic – check out his brother Jeon Junghun's Instagram drawings of BTS) and his sporting prowess, particularly in athletics, wresting and archery, would inspire BTS triumphs in successive Idol Star Athletics Championships. He was living up to the Golden *Maknae* name his leader had given him.

That isn't the only nickname Jungkook has picked up. As well as being affectionately called Kookie by fellow members and ARMY, you'll also catch him being called Nochu. This harks back to the *American Hustle Life* series when mentor Nate gave him a rap to copy, including the line 'Nochu ["Not you"], come thru'. Jungkook copied it so well, Nate gave him the name and it stuck.

Other names he has been called include Muscle Pig (and more recently Jeon Cena after the US wrestler John Cena, now himself a BTS fan), a flattering epithet based on his strength and his biceps; Bunny, after his beguiling smile that shows off his front teeth; Shining Prince, which Twitter took to after the *Love Yourself: Her* launch; and International Playboy, which he introduced himself as in an early documentary *Go! BTS*, ironically because at the time he seemed unable to even look a girl in the eye! Finally, some fans talk of Jungshook, a reference to the bemused and bewildered face that Kookie pulls in times of real confusion.

Such terms of endearment show how much members care for their youngest, but that doesn't stop them having fun at his expense. Jungkook's sixteenth birthday arrived on 1 September 2013. In a video on YouTube called 'BTS Surprise Birthday Party for Jung Kook!' we see the boys at a shoot for their trailer. During a break, Jungkook reads his fan mail and tries to enjoy 'Kookie Day', but the dance manager starts to criticize his dancing, and the others, hiding their laughter, join in. Poor Kookie is confused and a little upset, but they keep the pretence going right up until a beaming Suga emerges with a cake, candles and a song.

Not that he always reciprocates with the respect expected by his *hyungs*. Jungkook often pretends to be an evil *maknae*, teasing all the members with some excellent mimicry. Since debut, Jungkook has grown taller than Jimin and doesn't he let him know it! 'Calling me short and stroking my head – I'm two years older than you!' poor Jimin has been heard to complain! It seems Jimin can forgive Jungkook most things, though. He has said he reminds him of his younger brother and even when they're having fun there is a sense Jimin is looking out for Jungkook.

> Jungkook often pretends to be an evil *maknae*.

Although he's also two years older, V is very much capable of acting like a kid, too, and Kookie has remarked how similar his and V's personalities are, saying, 'He's random. Our comedic chords match well.' Jungkook and V also share a love of video games, especially *Overwatch*. In fact, Jungkook is the real games addict of the group (look for the scar on his left cheek, a souvenir of a fight with his brother over a game controller). At the end of 2016, when the group moved to a four-bedroom dorm, Jungkook won rock, paper, scissors to become the only member with his own room. He named it the golden closet and the other members always headed there when they were looking for a game.

When they upscaled again, he kept the name for his private recording studio. This is where he works on his covers, practises his piano playing, and it's also the home of Golden Closet Films (or G.C.F as it appears on YouTube), Jungkook's film studio. Releases so far, directed and edited by Jungkook, consist of short films of Jimin on a trip to Tokyo and of all the members having fun in Osaka. This showcases yet another of Kookie's talents, but one that hasn't yet spawned a nickname!

Jungkook is the least active of the group on Twitter. ARMY have encouraged him to post more and he has said he will try. He does, however, post his solo songs as gifts and as part of *Love Yourself: Tear* worked hard on writing and producing 'Magic Shop', a passionate fan song which he dedicated to ARMY. More than any other member of the group, Jungkook has grown up with BTS. The slight, shy, cute-as-anything adolescent has become a charismatic showman and a ripped hunk of a man – just witness his abs flash at the 2018 BBMAs – and the multi-talented Kookie has continued to reveal new skills. All credit to Big Hit for recognizing the potential in him, the Bangtans for raising a boy they can be proud of and, of course, to the Golden *Maknae* himself.

RM, Jimin and J-Hope looking effortlessly cool at the 2018 BBMAs.

Jungkook and V during a stunning performance of 'DNA' at the 2017 AMAs.

Jin and Jungkook being devastatingly handsome at the *Love Yourself: Her* launch in 2017.

SOPE! J-Hope and Suga performing on *Jimmy Kimmel Live!* in 2017.

Top: BTS using their platform for more charitable ventures, here promoting their LOVE MYSELF campaign, partnering with UNICEF to #ENDviolence against children and teenagers, Seoul, South Korea, November 2017.

Bottom: Taking a quick selfie break while visiting Music Choice in New York, USA, March 2017.

Top: *Daesang*! The boys cementing their position as South Korea's number-one act, here accepting the grand prize at the Seoul Music Awards in January 2018.

Bottom: At a press conference for the release of *Love Yourself: Tear*, Seoul, South Korea, May 2018.

J-Hope, Jungkook, V, Jin, RM, Suga and Jimin smouldering for the cameras in the *Love Yourself: Tear* concept photos, May 2018.

The boys returning to the BBMAs in Las Vegas, USA, in May 2018 to collect the award for 'Top Social Artist' for the second year in a row – and to put on a very special performance of 'Fake Love'. Here they are (clockwise from above) having fun on the red carpet, performing on stage, backstage with their trophy, and in the audience.

Top: BTS looking fashionable as ever in this photo released in June 2018 to celebrate the success of their Japanese-language album *Face Yourself*.

Bottom: A breathtaking performance of 'Fake Love' on *The Late Late Show with James Corden* in Los Angeles, USA, in June 2018, showing the world just how talented they really are – and how far they've come.

SEVENTEEN

DAESANG

n July 2016 BTS were still in Japan when the teaser pics went out for their second Japanese album. Released in September, *Youth* contained nine Japanese versions of their tracks, the single 'For You' and three new tracks. 'Introduction: Youth' is a rap intro and 'Good Day' a sweet vocal-line pop song, while 'Wishing on a Star' turned out to be a top favourite with ARMY around the world. A dreamy, mid-tempo song full of romantic echoes, the vocals are perfectly layered as it spells out the 'follow your dream whatever' message. *Youth* went straight to number one in the weekly and monthly Japanese charts, which was another first for BTS.

At the same time, something else was happening. Over nine days in early September, Big Hit uploaded a series of seven short (two- to three-minute) films to YouTube. Each film focused on a particular member, with Jungkook's film titled *Begin*, Jimin's *Lie*, V's *Stigma*, Suga's *First Love*, RM's *Reflection*, J-Hope's *Mama* and Jin's *Awake*.

They are each introduced by a brief narration in English voiced by RM and feature a backing track with excerpts from a new song. The films are heavily stylized and repeat key images from previous BTS videos, including fire, petals, baths and Polaroid photographs – it's like they planned it all along! Dark and heavy with symbolism, they convey feelings of alienation, self-doubt, angst and despair. Each of the members has a serious acting role and they rise to the occasion, filling their scenes with emotion and depth. The mood is easy to comprehend, but the exact meaning of each of the stories is open to interpretation and has, as a result, filled many pages of ARMY blogs and fan sites.

The key to understanding the films and much of the new comeback album could be found in the German writer Hermann Hesse's coming-of-age novel *Demian*.

In interviews, RM explained that the key to understanding the films and much of the new comeback album could be found in the German writer Hermann Hesse's coming-of-age novel, *Demian*, first published in 1919. Bang Si-hyuk had given them the story of a boy on the cusp of manhood, who is presented with a choice between light and darkness, safety and danger, good and evil, and must discover his own path. In the novel, the main character questions accepted values and rebels against a system that is frustrating and repressive. For BTS, it was a pretty inspired choice.

At the end of September 2016, Big Hit announced the date of the new album, *Wings*, and dropped a comeback trailer. Remember how the 'Save Me' video had signed off with the words 'BOY MEETS'? The trailer seemed to provide an answer as it was titled 'Boy Meets Evil'. Beginning with a quote from Hesse about shaking hands with the devil, it consists of J-Hope dancing to his own passionate rap.

J-Hope was the last of the rap line to get his own trailer/album opener, but his vocals are spot on – no swag, but rising and falling with intensity as he tells of temptation and of giving way to a love that is wrong but is too sweet to resist. Even more impressive is his dancing. Dressed in a long white shirt with ripped black jeans and new copper-coloured hair, J-Hope rips through a Dylan Mayoral-choreographed modern dance performance that is stunning in its expression and execution.

The concept photos soon followed. Matching all we had seen and heard in the past few weeks, the band moved away from their youthful, boyish image and instead embraced a more mature, sophisticated and elegant look. They wore crisp dress shirts and embroidered or floral jackets with plenty of velvet and satin. There were modern and vintage touches such as chokers and ruffled necklines, single feathers, cuffed jeans and flower appliqués. Although their hair was still multi-coloured, it was more muted and chic, too.

> The band moved away from their youthful, boyish image and instead embraced a more mature, sophisticated and elegant look.

The music video for the comeback was for a new track, 'Blood, Sweat & Tears', released on 10 October. It was an ambitious work combining drama and dance as well as incorporating the symbolism and ideas of the short films. Continuing the theme of the concept photos, we are taken into an opulent world of high art as the guys enter a museum filled with classical statues and paintings. They are dressed in Saint Laurent and Dolce & Gabbana finery, and they look foppish, bohemian and absolutely stunning.

The dramatic section of the video gradually builds a feeling of innocence being left behind, of a yielding to temptation and of a falling. The group play out this narrative in various scenes leading up to Jin kissing the statue. All around are artworks reinforcing this story, including Herbert James Draper's painting of Icarus, Michelangelo's sculpture of the Virgin Mary holding the dead body of Jesus Christ, and *The Fall of the Rebel Angels* painting by Pieter Bruegel the Elder.

Yet this is a K-pop group. They are not supposed to be delving into the world of art and philosophy any more than they were supposed to be questioning their education and career expectations in 'No More Dream'. Not content to write 'boy meets girl' lyrics, they are exploring ideas of what adulthood, and the choices it presents, means to them. It certainly provides food for thought for the viewer.

Except they also manage to distract many ARMY from such issues with their performance and choreography. This is by far the most deliberate attempt by the group to show a sexy and alluring side and, judging by the comments on YouTube, they completely smash it. The mood is created by heavy eyeliner, low necklines, chokers and soft lips while the dance retains the trademark razor-sharp moves but incorporates sensual glances, self-caresses and body movements. Add moments such as Jungkook licking his finger or Jimin's naked shoulder-revealing jacket flip and the video no doubt left millions around the world too stunned to intellectually engage.

While the video racked up more than 6 million views in under twenty-four hours, BTS were at the same time launching *Wings*, their second full-length BTS album. Just as the record is about youth growing and flying, so it is about the group's individual members spreading their own wings. On this album every member gets their own solo track, which, with the exception of Jungkook, is a song they wrote themselves. This is an extraordinary achievement, not only for the members themselves, but also for Big Hit, as groups controlled by the big three companies are rarely given such trust and freedom.

The fifteen tracks on *Wings* embrace a host of synth styles, including up-to-the-minute sounds of tropical house, moombahton and even neo-soul. It begins with the J-Hope rap 'Boy Meets Evil' used for the trailer, and 'Blood, Sweat & Tears', which puts the spotlight on Jimin

BANGTAN BOMB

'BLOOD SWEAT & TEARS' MV REACTION BY BTS

If the symbol-searching and intellectual workout of the *Wings* short films and the 'Blood, Sweat & Tears' music video leave you exhausted, then search out this Bangtan bomb on YouTube. It shows the boys getting their first view of the music video. You won't find much to help you with the meaning, but there is plenty to smile about as they coo, cheer and whoop at each other's dance moves, acting and general sexiness.

as he opens the track with a beautifully breathless, high-pitched vocal. To a luxuriously layered backing track of chimes, sirens and claps, the vocal line excels harmonically with the most infectious of hooks. Within the lyrics of this apparent love song, there is also something darker that alludes to the theme of the album. As RM explained in their concept launch, 'The harder a temptation is to resist, the more you think about it and vacillate. That uncertainty is part of the process of growing. ['Blood Sweat & Tears'] is a song that shows how one thinks, chooses and grows.'

The next section of *Wings* is taken up by the seven solo efforts of the group. These have the same titles as their short films. Jungkook goes first with 'Begin', a slow R&B track that he eases into a Bieberesque-style as he recalls his arrival in Seoul at fifteen years old and how his relationship with his 'brothers' in the group grew so strong. Next, Jimin takes the mic for his track, 'Lie', switching from sultry to emotional in a tour-de-force vocal accompanied by haunting orchestral strings, screeches, jarred instruments and eerie backing vocals. In contrast, to a classic instrumental beat, V's 'Stigma' plays out bass-heavy vocals, whispers and even near-screams in a sometimes spine-tingling, guilt-laden song of hurt.

'First Love' is classic Suga. An original and honest rap, he uses the tone of his spoken voice, rising from calm to impassioned to frame a hymn to his childhood piano. He later admitted crying while recording it. The rap line's contributions continue with RM's 'Reflection', a calm state-of-mind take on life's contradictions. Written while sitting in the very Ttukseom Park he raps about, it begins with his own phone recording of the sound of the passing subway.

J-Hope revealed that at a group meeting he announced that he intended to write a song about his mother and that it would be bright and 'Hope'-ful. True to his word, a jaunty, jazzy track backs his poem about mother and son love. The lyrics are beautiful in both their simplicity and detail, right down to the naming of the restaurants in which she worked, and the lovely gesture of including her voice saying 'Hello'.

Jin claims Suga originally thought a ballad-type song wouldn't fit the album, but the last soloist's track proved to be a favourite of all the group. A conventional slow number with an orchestral and piano backing, 'Awake' gorgeously showcases Jin's control and vocal range as he sings a song of heart-rending self-doubt and heart-warming self-motivation.

The group songs take over again with 'Lost', an upbeat track that throws the vocal line's voices against each other in deft contrast as they sing a message of hope. A partly RM-written coming-of-age track, it speaks of the difficulty of choosing your path in life and of believing in yourself to find the right way. This is followed by the traditional rappers' track, 'Cypher Pt. 4', which contains the usual statements addressed to their haters, but this time sounds confident and assertive (the 'I love myself' repetition especially), with none of the defensiveness and staged hip-hop arrogance that has flavoured some previous cyphers.

The next track is 'Am I Wrong'. The first surprise is that it begins with a sample of a song by Grammy Award-winning blues singer Keb' Mo' from 1994. The second is that BTS make it their own, retaining the blues feel, but transforming it into a high-energy dance pop track with the hookiest of choruses. Talk about pushing the boundaries! The third of the tracks performed at promotions, '21st Century Girls', follows on nicely. Its driving beat, fun and relatively simple choreography and call-and-respond lyrics make it an automatic crowd-pleaser. What's more, the lyrics show how BTS have progressed. The somewhat narrow male view of 'War of Hormone' has been replaced by a celebration of women for what and who they are. It's a heartening 'girl power' anthem that says 'love yourself' and, hey, it has the funkiest vibe, too.

And they keep coming: 'Two! Three! (Still Wishing for More Good Days)' was specifically written for ARMY. This first official fan anthem has a charming rap and vocal mix, a comforting message that we'll get through the hard times together, and a chant tailor-made for singalongs at concerts. The album concludes with 'Interlude: Wings', a poppy Jungkook-led dance track that encapsulates the wings metaphor of embracing adulthood, facing the challenges and obstacles, but following the path you choose.

The album was released in four versions: W, I, N and G. They share the same black cover with a smoke pattern and the *Wings* logo of four differently shaded circles. The versions differ in the photo and lyric books included, as they follow the theme of the 'Blood, Sweat & Tears' video and the short films by pairing up the members and leaving Jin as a lone figure. The photobook of *W* features glorious colour shots of Jin as well as group photos; *I* also has group pictures but features J-Hope and V; *N* focuses on Jimin and Suga; leaving *G* to RM and Jungkook. They do, however, each come with a completely random Polaroid.

Their first comeback stage came on 13 October (Jin's birthday) on Mnet's *M Countdown*, where they performed '21st Century Girls' in casual wear, followed by 'Am I Wrong' in different-coloured suit jackets, before appearing on a 'museum' set dressed in their sophisticated get-up for 'Blood, Sweat & Tears'. From the online reaction to the

BANGTAN BOMB

BTS 21ST CENTURY GIRL DANCE PRACTICE (HALLOWEEN VER.)

This is possibly the most error-strewn BTS dance practice ever, but go easy on them. It's Halloween and these boys love to dress up. It can't be easy doing the moves when you're costumed as a giant rabbit (Jungkook), a huge vegetable (Jimin) or a pantomime horse (Jin). We also have Suga in Hanbok (traditional Korean clothing), J-Hope as a skeleton, V channelling manga character Syaoran and RM, of course, dresses as Ryan the lovable cartoon lion (his obsession – he even has Ryan pyjamas).

performances and songs, it was no surprise when the following weeks saw them pick up trophies on *Show Champion*, *M Countdown*, *Music Bank* (two weeks running), *Inkigayo* and *The Show Choice*.

Wings was clearly BTS's most ambitious work yet: a collection of fifteen songs spanning music genres, composers, lyrical ideas and performers. They had been nervous about how it would be received, Jin revealing that he had had difficulty sleeping before the comeback, but from the day of release it was obvious it was going to be massively popular. Tracks from the album soon dominated the domestic charts, the album itself became the year's highest-selling title on the Gaon charts and within four days of release, 'Blood, Sweat & Tears' had achieved the cherished 'all-kill', topping all eight Korean music charts.

It was truly astounding. Around the world, BTS were making headlines, too. The single ranked number one on the iTunes charts in twenty-three countries, including Canada, Brazil, New Zealand, Singapore and Norway, as well as on the Chinese equivalent. It went straight to the top of the Billboard World Digital Song Sales chart. The album was hot internationally as well: BTS became the first Korean act to break into the UK album charts at number sixty-two, while in addition to the above-mentioned countries, Finland, Sweden, Ireland and the Netherlands all saw *Wings* making an impact on the charts.

North America had seen K-pop acts perform well before, but nothing compared to this. Canada had fallen for BTS big time. The album broke into the top twenty, while 'Blood, Sweat & Tears' set a K-pop record at number eighty-six. Meanwhile, in the USA they were not only storming the album charts

> They were not only storming the album charts like no other Korean group ever before but receiving critical acclaim, too.

like no other Korean group ever before (reaching twenty-six on the Billboard 200 chart), but receiving critical acclaim, too. *Rolling Stone* named *Wings* 'one of the most conceptually and sonically ambitious pop albums of 2016', while another high-profile magazine, *Fuse*, listed it as the eighth-best album of 2016, applauding its 'fascinating concepts and wholly accessible productions that don't sound out of place on top forty radio'. Wow!

Once again BTS were determined to debut the performances of the new tracks to their fans. As November brought their third fan meeting at the massive Gocheok Sky Dome baseball stadium in Seoul, it presented the perfect opportunity. ARMY snapped up the 38,000 tickets for the two days in minutes and they were not disappointed as the group held question-and-answer sessions, performed old hits (including 'kindergarten' versions by J-Hope, Jin and V), Jimin made his rap debut alongside Suga, the boys showed off their new choreographies and gave their individual thanks to the fans. And no one who was there will ever forget V's tribute to his recently deceased grandmother (accompanied by Jungkook's tears) or ARMY's goosebump-raising singing of 'Two! Three! ...', their new anthem.

Back in the summer, the group had shared a visit to BoMunSa temple on Seokmodo Island in South Korea. There, in common with many tourists, the guys had carved a prayer on a tile. On it they asked for *Wings* to be a *daebak* or great success. It was beginning to look like their prayers had been answered.

With award season about to begin, you could forgive them for thinking their dream of the ultimate prize, the *daesang*, might be around the corner. Good news or bad, they didn't have to hold their breath for long in order to find out. On 19 November 2016 they were back in the Gocheok Sky Dome for the Melon Music Awards. With

EXO picking up the Artist of the Year award, many, including BTS, expected them to scoop up the best album *daesang*, too. So when *The Most Beautiful Moment in Life: Young Forever* was announced as the winner, the shocked look on the boys' faces was priceless. RM stood up, but the rest of the group remained seated, looking at each other with open eyes and gaping mouths. V walked to the stage, asking in disbelief, 'It's us? Us?' and RM had to compose himself before making his thank-you speech to ARMY, Big Hit and the members' families. At this point Jin was sobbing and J-Hope was forced to wipe away his own tears. The group hug before they left the stage was brimming with joy, relief and togetherness. They had worked so hard in the last three years and it meant so much to them to finally be recognized like this.

A couple of weeks later, on 2 December, they not only attended the MAMA ceremony in Hong Kong, but completely owned the stage with their performance. From Jungkook suspended in mid-air to J-Hope's solo 'Boy Meets Evil' dance, to his and a blindfolded Jimin's extraordinary mirrored dance, and the spellbinding group choreography of 'Blood, Sweat & Tears', they left the fans in no doubt as to who the artist of the year was. And MAMA were ready to confirm the truth with just that award – their second *daesang* in as many weeks. Their emotional response was just as strong as at the MMAs, with RM struggling to start his speech and this time Jungkook and Suga finding it impossible to fight back the tears.

Their second *daesang* in as many weeks.

In his acceptance speech, RM explained that they had been through so much since they debuted and that, although many had doubted they could make it, ARMY had believed in them and helped them fulfil their dreams. He ended with a wish: that in 2017 they might fly ever higher on their beautiful wings.

EIGHTEEN

ARMY: TEAMWORK MAKES THE DREAM WORK

BTS fans are as instrumental to the group's massive success as any of the members. They not only purchase the albums, download the tracks and buy up concert tickets in record time, but they provide a constant stream of love, support and encouragement to the boys. That's why, in almost every interview they do and every speech they make, BTS declare their affection for and gratitude to ARMY. Take what RM said when the band won the coveted *daesang* at the 2018 Seoul Music Awards: 'The reason at the end is always all of you. Thank you for being the reason we can do this work. We'll try to be even a small bit of help for you in your life. Thank you, ARMY!' He couldn't have made it clearer: BTS appreciate ARMY.

On 9 July 2013, a month after their debut, BTS announced that their official fan club would be called ARMY. It fitted well with the name Bulletproof Boy Scouts and, as noted earlier, had its own meaning: Adorable Representative MC for Youth. Just like the group themselves, BTS's fans would speak out for their generation. This announcement was made through their online

> BTS's fans would speak out for their generation.

fan café (cafe.daum.net/BANGTAN), a forum most K-pop groups use to communicate with fans and encourage discussion. It's still an important place for finding out about what BTS are up to, but it's largely in Korean. However, translations in many languages are posted almost instantly on Twitter, so international fans need not be left behind.

For a small fee the official fan club offers a chance to attend fan meetings, priority booking for concerts and other benefits. It is, however, still largely aimed at Korean fans and has set recruitment periods (usually in May) and limits on the number of new members accepted at any one time. However, you don't need to be a member to call yourself ARMY, because simply loving, supporting and following the group is enough.

BTS certainly make it easy to follow them. The top social artist awards won by BTS at the Billboard Music Awards in both 2017 and 2018 confirm that no other group and their fans have the same level of connection. They are in daily contact on Twitter from their shared handle @BTS_twt, which the boys themselves tweet from; @BTS_bighit is the official account run by Big Hit Entertainment. English speakers can also follow them on the impressive translation service provided by @BTS_Trans. They frequently broadcast live messages, skits or even whole concerts on the V-Live app, and the BANGTANTV channel on YouTube uploads numerous videos of performances, dance practices, backstage footage and the sometimes silly and often hilarious Bangtan bombs. Their Instagram account,

> The top social artist awards won by BTS at the BBMAs in both 2017 and 2018 confirm that no other group and their fans have the same level of connection.

@bts.bighitofficial, is full of messages from and photos of the group, and their Facebook page 'Bangtan.official' carries similar posts.

It's difficult to estimate just how many ARMY there are. There are the 20 or so million who viewed 'Fake Love' on its first day on YouTube (and that's accounting for two views each). There are the 30-plus million who voted in the BBMAs, and the 25 million followers of the official Twitter and translation accounts. We're certainly talking more people than the population of Australia and one thing is certain: you're never alone with ARMY.

Surveys revealed where most ARMY lived and, unexpectedly, the Philippines came out top, with South Korea only second, followed by Indonesia, Vietnam, Thailand, Malaysia, Brazil and then the USA. However, the fan base is growing fast around the world, especially in Europe and the Americas.

Twitter has emerged as ARMY's favourite channel. In 2016, BTS became the first K-pop group to receive their own Twitter emoji, the bulletproof vest, which was updated to reflect the new logo in 2017. Twitter is instrumental in spreading the word. Any news about the group and every comment or post from them is retweeted countless times. In December 2017, the band received Twitter Asia's 'golden tweet' of the year, with a video that exceeded 1 million engagements: 778,000 likes and 374,000 retweets. What was it? A thirteen-second clip of an unseen member putting a French fry into the mouth of a sleeping Jungkook!

The really great thing about ARMY is that they are not a passive force; they are constantly finding new ways to support BTS. Hashtags to celebrate members' birthdays, to congratulate them and to send them get-well notes are common, but ARMY are capable of getting random messages trending too, such as #ThankYouJungkook, which appeared in January 2018 and was followed by similar messages to the other members.

Other support is practical. Among many examples is RM's collaboration with Wale, which came about after fans got in touch with the US rapper, or the successful lobbying of radio station DJs, such as BBC Radio One's Adele Roberts, in order to persuade them to play BTS tracks. A campaign which began in September 2017 when fans posted pictures of V with a Coca-Cola can resulted in the group being appointed as official football World Cup 2018 ambassadors for the soft drink. ARMY are clever, too: they urged fans not to buy J-Hope's mixtape *Hope World* on its release date, having worked out that delaying by a day would result in a higher ranking in the Billboard charts.

Of course, the most practical support ARMY give BTS is through voting. Whether it's for TV music shows or national and international awards, fans' online votes help determine the winner and ARMY help to get every possible BTS vote out through reminders, hashtags and encouragement. The BBMAs' top social artist award is determined solely by public voting and this is where ARMY have really come into their own. In 2018 they broke the Guinness World Record they had set the previous year as they generated 51.72 million tweets for the hashtag #IVoteBTSBBMAs.

Just like their idols, ARMY also look to see how they can help in the wider world. Instances of local ARMY groups arranging charity donations are numerous. They can be traditional rice donations to bring good luck to BTS concerts, or responses to emergencies in places like Nepal where local ARMY organized

> Just like their idols, ARMY also look to see how they can help in the wider world.

collection points to raise money and gather emergency supplies for flood victims. Often these gestures are in honour of individual BTS members, so in the US a donation was given to Save the Children in Suga's name, in Peru ARMY celebrated Jungkook's twenty-first birthday by 'adopting' an endangered pygmy rabbit, and Korean fans adopted five whales to mark one of RM's birthdays.

Perhaps the most widely publicized example was ARMY's participation in a 2018 campaign run by the organization Star Wars: Force for Change. Every time people used the hashtag #RoarForChange on social media, Star Wars: Force for Change pledged to donate one US dollar to support UNICEF. Knowing UNICEF was BTS's chosen charity, US TV news reporter George Pennacchio enlisted ARMY's help and in just a few hours ARMY had mustered enough tweets to help raise the maximum million-dollar donation.

Away from the fan clubs and social media, ARMY have their own thriving sites. Amino, Allkpop and Bangtan Base are some of the best. Here you'll find reviews, comments and theories, especially on the meaning of the videos, but also in-depth analysis of songs, clothes, hair and just about every aspect of each BTS member. The discussions are often the result of detailed research or diligent translation and they make for fascinating reading. Naturally, ARMY themselves like to get creative and there are some excellent drawings of the group on these sites. There are also lots of fanfiction sites, but beware, because these are not always of the highest quality and the content can be unsuitable or even upsetting for younger ARMY.

An exception to this was *Outcast*, a fanfic which appeared on Twitter in January 2018. This story, told by @flirtaus across a series of 'text messages', began with a fictional exchange between J-Hope and Suga over a missing person and developed to include all the members. It took the form of a five-night survival game where fans voted every night for their favourite resolution to the cliffhanger, with over 300,000 following the story.

Also on Twitter, in autumn 2017, a dance group called the Williams Fam posted their own choreography for sections of the BTS song 'Go Go'. When BTS themselves retweeted, the Fam decided to issue a Go Go Challenge, inspiring ARMY around the world to share their own attempts. What's fantastic about this vibrant online community is that all ARMY get to take part and feel a connection to BTS. After all, only the very fortunate have the chance to attend the fan meets, *festa* gatherings or hi-touch sessions, but as BTS embark on a world tour in 2018 and 2019, hopefully there will be opportunities for thousands more to see the Bangtan Boys in person.

Those who haven't witnessed a K-pop concert before find BTS live shows astounding, with a degree of audience participation unheard of in the US or Europe. BTS put their heart and soul into their shows. Performances regularly exceed two hours as they run specially made videos, perform a carefully selected set of old favourites and new songs, take in changes of stage costume and engage with their audience. And it's the audience members that take the experience to a new level with chants, light sticks and banners.

And it's the audience members that take the [concert] experience to a new level with chants, light sticks and banners.

The most common fan chant is one that calls out the names of the members. It's usually chanted at the beginning of songs or sometimes in instrumental breaks. It's important to chant the names in the correct order – 'Kim Namjoon! Kim Seokjin! Min Yoongi! Jung Hoseok! Park

Jimin! Kim Taehyung! Jeon Jungkook!' – and just as important to finish with a shout of 'BTS!' Other chants take the form of echoes of words or phrases in the songs or responses to set phrases. There are fan chants for most of the songs with the exception of solo numbers, but the name of the member singing is often chanted during breaks. If you're lucky enough to have a ticket to a BTS concert, it's definitely worth checking out the chants on YouTube (the Mnet K-pop channel is a good place to start) beforehand and practising, although if you don't get a chance, the 'BTS!' chant is one that anyone can join in with.

Anyone new to K-pop might be intrigued to see the thousands of dots of lights emanating from the audience and even more amazed when they change colour simultaneously. The light stick is a K-pop must-have accessory. Each group has their own colour and BTS lay claim to silver-grey. The official BTS light stick is called an ARMY bomb and has a spherical globe at the end of a short handle. The light can be set to remain on, to flash or to dim, and when at a concert a Bluetooth connection synchronizes the colour of the light with the stage lights. The effect is breathtaking.

ARMY across the globe come up with their own special ways of connecting with the group. They distribute banners, spell out messages with light sticks or even change lyrics to express their love for the group. These projects are often organized through local Twitter groups or on the day by dedicated ARMY, who hand out slogan cards or printed instructions on how to join in.

All these activities help strengthen the bond between ARMY and BTS at a live show, but there is one song above all that brings them together. The song 'Two! Three! (Still Wishing for More Good Days)' is BTS's present to ARMY and when it's played live it's the cue for ARMY to join in – and they often continue even after the music has finished! BTS and ARMY are inseparable; they inspire and support each other. This is a group who will never forget their ARMY and a fan base that is totally loyal and devoted. As BTS become ever more successful, so ARMY becomes stronger and works ever harder to support them. As BTS themselves would say: '*Hwaiting!*'

> BTS and ARMY are inseparable; they inspire and support each other.

BANGTAN BOMB

BTS '고민보다 GO' STAGE WITH ARMY ~PERFECT VOICE~

If you need proof of the special relationship ARMY have with BTS, just watch this bomb. As the boys record their comeback stage singing 'Go Go', ARMY are in full attendance. Wielding lightsticks and accompanying the song with well-drilled chants, they are a vital part of the show – and don't BTS just know it. Their words of gratitude from the stage show just how much they appreciate ARMY's dedication.

NINETEEN

WINGS OVER AMERICA

n their 2016 Christmas message on V-Live, BTS harked back to 'A Typical Trainee's Christmas', the hardship song they had recorded four years previously. For a second it suddenly seemed to dawn on them how far they had come. And when they recalled the letters they had posted from Santa Claus Village in Finland, those who could remember what they wrote (the letters hadn't arrived yet!), revealed they had wished for a *daesang*. Now here they were six months later with two!

On 19 January 2017, despite taking home the most awards of the night at the Seoul Music Awards, including a *bonsang* (best album) for *Wings*, best music video for 'Blood, Sweat & Tears' and best male dance performance, they missed out to EXO on the Awards' big one, the *daesang*. It had been a similar story at the Golden Disc Awards a few days earlier, but no matter. Nothing stays still in Bangtanland.

BTS were headline news now, with all the scoops that went along with the fame. In January, it was reported that BTS and Big Hit Entertainment had secretly donated a substantial sum to charities connected to the families of the 2014 Sewol Ferry Disaster. The ferry had sunk, killing over 300 people, most of them high-school students on their way to a field trip on Jeju Island, a favourite destination for

BTS. Each member had donated ₩10 million (around $8,500) and Big Hit had added some ₩100 million ($85,000). Why the secret? It was simply that they hadn't donated in order to get publicity; it was just something they wanted to do.

Now it was time for a mini-comeback. The concept photos were a shift in mood from *Wings*. Altogether more relaxed, as multicoloured confetti fell, the group posed in front of a paint-splattered old building or were pictured in a bus shelter, silhouetted against blue sea and sky. They were happy, in colourful casual wear, and some of the group had been at the hair dye again, with Suga sporting blue streaks, RM a purple wash and Jimin fluffy candy-floss pink.

On 13 February they dropped a new four-track mini-album called *Wings: You Never Walk Alone*. In a sixty-minute preview show on V-Live – much of it taken up by a hilarious game of Twister – they explained that the casual and younger look (J-Hope now had yellow-blond hair) was to reflect the new stories they were telling in this special continuation of *Wings*. The four new tracks were all written by members of the group which, they said, were messages of consolation and hope.

Just over an hour later, the music video for one of those tracks, 'Spring Day', was released. Once again they were pushing boundaries with the music as an indie rock style permeated the regular beats and EDM sound. It was not their catchiest song, but the vocal line filled the melody with so much emotion that it still makes a strong impression.

The video, a beautifully filmed piece full of dreamy pastel colours and contrasting bright and muted light, includes a train journey, a mountain of clothes, Jimin carrying someone's sneakers and a hotel called Omelas, a reference

Once again they were pushing boundaries with the music.

to a short story by Ursula K. Le Guin, in which the happiness of the inhabitants of a city with that name depends on the perpetual misery of a single child. Naturally ARMY came up with lots of fascinating theories about what it all meant. When asked whether the song hinted at the Sewol Ferry tragedy, RM, who had written the lyrics with Suga, admitted he had read that suggestion, but said, 'Every viewer can have a different interpretation of the music or the music video, because it depends on their mind, so we wish to leave this open.'

'Spring Day' was an immediate 'all-kill', the number of downloads actually crashing the Melon site. It swept to number one in thirteen different countries' iTunes charts and hit number eight in the US iTunes chart, making BTS the first-ever K-pop band to break into the top ten.

> 'Spring Day' was an immediate 'all-kill', the number of downloads actually crashing the Melon site.

As the world was still digesting this latest offering, BTS put out another explosive track. In direct contrast to the previous week's hit, 'Not Today' was a riotous demonstration of power and energy. The music video focused on the choreography, although Big Hit also posted an eight-minute dance video, in which, supported by a fifty-strong black-hoodie-clad dance army, BTS switch from elegant moves to lightning-fast jerks and jumps with military precision in another Keone Madrid masterpiece. A compelling and stirring up-tempo dance fest, it cries out that we might lose in the future but not today; today we fight back.

You Never Walk Alone was released in two versions containing different sets of photos. The pink 'right' version has a photo of the paint-stained old building, while the green 'left' version has a picture of the empty bus shelter. Of course, the books were packed with sumptuous shots from the respective photoshoots and had the usual accompanying random photocards and posters.

In addition to the two released tracks there were two other new songs on the album. 'Interlude: Wings' had been given a remix, a dance break and a new J-Hope verse to become 'Outro: Wings', while the final track on the album is a completely new song. 'A Supplementary Story: You Never Walk Alone' spells out the message of this second part. A laid-back rap and vocal BTS-style track in which Suga and J-Hope even sing some of their rap lines, it offers a reassuring note after the harsh truths highlighted by many of the other songs. If we stick together, it says, we will be okay.

The 2017 BTS Live Trilogy Episode III: The Wings Tour began on

BANGTAN BOMB

BTS'S '봄날' WON @ MUSIC BANK (FEAT. 봄날 NEW DANCE BY JIN)

BTS only promoted 'Spring Day' for a week, but nevertheless managed to capture four music-show awards. This bomb shows backstage footage from the third of those victories, at *Music Bank*. The thanks to ARMY are heartfelt and fun, but the real attraction is in the second part of the bomb, where we see Jin's attempts to choreograph a 'Spring Day' dance to end the show. If you want to see what it looked like when they perform it for real you'll find that elsewhere on YouTube.

18 and 19 February with two shows at their new 'home', the Gocheok Sky Dome in Seoul. During the set, they broke so that each member could personally thank the fans for the *daesang* which, they stressed, they had won together. Suga poetically said how BTS were one wing and ARMY were another, so together they could fly; Jin joked how his handsomeness must be contagious, as over the years it had spread to the others; and RM talked of how he read ARMY's letters and felt they were walking together into the future. But it was J-Hope who set the tears flowing; he revealed it was his birthday (that much they already knew!) and said how privileged he was that his mother was there to hear his solo track, a song dedicated to her.

In March, they took the tour to the Americas. First port of call: Chile. When they played Chile in 2015 they had sold seats for half of the Moviestar Arena. This time they would play to the whole arena and, when that sold out almost immediately, they hastily booked a second concert. The Beatlemania-type scenes at the airport on their arrival, outside their hotel in Santiago and at the arena, showed Chilean ARMY to be as passionate as any in the world.

Chilean support for [BTS] surpassed support for groups such as One Direction.

The *New York Times* even wrote an article about how Chilean support for the Korean group surpassed support for groups such as One Direction. RM explained, 'We talk about our own turmoil and mental breakdowns as honestly as possible in the music ... We believe Chilean fans tend to connect to those values, maybe a little deeper than fans in other countries.'

On a diversion from the tour, BTS hit Mexico City to open the first ever KCON in Latin America and that was pretty wild, too. ARMY linked hands to form their own guard of honour at the airport and the band set the arena rocking with a set of hits, before playing KCON's Piñata Time game, in which they responded to tasks selected by an on-screen cartoon piñata, including blowing kisses at the audience and making a series of photoshoot poses for fans.

An estimated 8,000 ARMY were there to meet them at the airport in Brazil; in fact, so many fans turned up that the boys had to sneak out through a back door! Considering the Citibank Hall venue had a capacity of only 7,000, there were sure to be some disappointed fans, but those who made it to the concerts witnessed something really special. The group would later tell the Distractify website that the fans' synchronized dancing was a highlight of the tour: 'Hundreds of fans were dancing with us behind the seats like a flash mob,' they said. 'It was awesome!'

One particular moment lives on in BTS history. In RM's solo 'Reflection', he sings a recurring line about how he wishes he could love himself. Every time he did so on the first night in São Paulo, ARMY would reply in deafening tones: 'We love you!' The next night, revealing that he had heard ARMY's cries, he changed the lyrics to 'Yes, I do love myself.' In the BTS social media world, word travels fast. By the next concert and for the rest of the tour, it was a special moment that would be replayed between RM and ARMY again and again around the world. Thanks Brazil!

In 2017 *Run BTS!* returned with some more choice episodes. 'High School Skit' (episode eleven) finds the guys drawing lots to determine their roles in a high-school drama, resulting in a nerdy V, emo J-Hope and a nice-but-dim RM competing to win the heart of a new female student, memorably played by Suga! Episode twenty-three is another must-see. BTS all love their dogs so it's a special treat when they are each paired up with a canine friend. After each dog chooses a member,

BANGTAN BOMB

JUNGKOOK WENT TO HIGH SCHOOL WITH BTS FOR GRADUATION! – BTS (방탄소년단)

Awww! The *maknae* looks so cute in his graduation uniform as he picks up his high-school certificate. And if his solo track 'Begin' doesn't make his love for his fellow members abundantly clear, take a look at his excitement at them attending his ceremony – and his gleeful anticipation of the celebration meal of black bean noodles!

they spend time bonding before competing in a series of trials. It's just amazing to watch the chemistry and affection that develops between the boys and their dogs in such a short time.

You also have to look up episode thirty-one in which they play games from old variety shows. Non-Korean viewers might find this confusing, but fast-forward to halfway through where they play the 'Half-asleep game' in which they have to sleep for thirty minutes and, on waking, remember a children's song, in this case 'The Cool Tomato Song'. We see them in their pyjamas, in deep sleep – Jungkook doesn't really wake up even when he falls out of his inflatable bed! – and then they're woken and have to sing. It really is BTS gold.

BTS Gayo also returned with more games and challenges. They had a relay to draw pictures of K-pop songs, a K-pop quiz, and had to guess and sing children's songs. Track fifteen is the real highlight.

Shot entirely in a hotel while in Chile on the *Wings* tour, the group are challenged to make their own music video. With RM as director, Jungkook on camera and Jin as choreographer, they shoot an MV for 'Spine Breaker' in their rooms, the restaurant and even the elevator. The result is not exactly 'DNA', but it's a whole lot of fun in the making!

Having achieved their long-cherished dream of a *daesang*, BTS's new goal lay thousands of miles away. They wanted success in the US. They wanted Billboard chart glory and to fill stadiums like Beyoncé and Bieber. They were already on their way. They'd hit the Billboard 200, as well as the iTunes singles chart top ten, but further proof of American interest came before the tour when Wale and RM collaborated on the politically charged rap single 'Change'.

> BTS's new goal lay thousands of miles away. They wanted success in the US.

When their dates in Newark, New Jersey, on 23 March and Anaheim, California, on 1 April sold out in hours, it even took their tour promoters by surprise. Another night at each venue was quickly added and they squeezed a night in Chicago in between as they realized just how popular this K-pop act had become. All in all, 60,000 seats across the country were sold. 'We always hoped we could be popular in America, but we thought it was all a dream,' RM told the *Orange County Weekly* before the show in Anaheim. 'Even after we heard about Billboard, we didn't know that we could be a sold-out artist for five nights. So, it's like, "Ok, what's happening right now?" And everyone [in the group] thinks that they should learn English now!'

With the exception of RM, their English did not improve substantially, but they all made an effort to communicate with the fans. In Chicago, Jungkook announced, 'We are far, far away, but we will always be together', and RM took some pleasure in pointing out that he had practised that line 'a million times', but the lack of fluency certainly didn't stop them from developing a fabulous rapport with ARMY across the country.

'We actually were scared of performing in America as a solo act,' RM told the *Orange County Register*. 'But after we were on stage our fear disappeared. The fans are like friends. Singing along to all of the lyrics even through the raps.' American ARMY even developed their own way of demonstrating their affection. After the group finished the set, they accompanied their pleas for an encore by covering their light sticks and phone lights with coloured plastic bags, sometimes distributed in advance by fans, which created an incredible rainbow effect across the concert hall.

> The sheer energy and step-perfect synchronization over a draining two-hour show was incredible.

For those in the audience used to watching US acts perform, the performances were eye-opening. Not only was the bond between die-hard fans and the group unlike anything they had seen before, but the sheer energy and step-perfect synchronization over a draining two-hour show was incredible. No wonder hundreds of merely curious concert-goers left the venues as converted fans.

BTS left American shores to take the *Wings* tour to Asia to visit Thailand, Indonesia, the Philippines and Hong Kong – all to the same rapturous welcome. Just a few weeks later, on 21 May, they were back in the States, this time in Las Vegas, on the red, or rather magenta, carpet, for the Billboard Music Awards. Their presence meant they were officially being noticed, even if many people didn't recognize them, as was made apparent when Jin received comments on Twitter about his good looks under the hashtag #ThirdOneFromTheLeft.

The BBMAs is one of the major music award ceremonies in the USA and a K-pop group had never been nominated for – let alone won – an award before, so BTS's bewilderment at winning the top social artist award, a fan-voted honour which had been won by Justin Bieber for the previous six years, was understandable. Breaking all previous records, BTS had racked up a staggering 300 million online votes to take the award – many fans no doubt voting more than once.

Along with many others across the States, some US artists were beginning to realize what the BTS deal was all about. Halsey and The Chainsmokers were pictured with them at the awards, Suga revealed he had met rapper Drake, and V boasted that when Celine Dion had heard V was a long-time fan, she invited the group to her concert. Others declaring themselves fans included singer Camila Cabello, who tweeted, 'They r soooo sweet', and actors Ansel Elgort and Laura Marano.

> BTS had racked up a staggering 300 million online votes.

Still on a high a few days later, BTS were able to thank some of ARMY in person when, on 26 May, they took the *Wings* tour to Sydney, Australia. It was their second visit Down Under, but it was apparent as soon as they touched down that their fan base had multiplied. Tickets had sold out within hours and the crowd at the Qudos Bank Arena was six times the size of their Red Bullet audience.

One member of the group has a special affection for Australia. When he was young, RM spent some time there with family and the first words he uttered on stage were, 'G'day mate!' Later, he reprised his Australian accent and closed the concert by saying, 'You know, I must say that you guys live in such a beautiful country. I went to the

Opera House yesterday and I saw people sitting on the grass, and the sea and the wind – it was so, so legit. So if I can't live in Korea I want to live in Australia!' The Aussie fans savoured every second of the concert, reacting with hysterical screams to the solo stages, the latest hits and the 'rocket through the history of BTS' medley (© Jin). The Bangtan Boys had, if not conquered, then at least secured a foothold in yet another country.

On 29 May 2017, they made a triumphant return to Seoul, pausing for a press conference in which they posed in their magenta carpet suits with their BBMA trophy and spoke modestly about their incredible success in the US. Inevitably, the question of how far they would go to progress in America was raised, as it would be many times over the next year. Would they record a song in English? RM's reply was that they weren't planning to officially debut in the States, because they wanted to carry on doing what they did best. He said, 'We want to continue to rap in Korean and do things that only BTS can do, rather than switching gears to suit a new market.' Integrity had always been an essential characteristic of BTS; it was reassuring to ARMY everywhere that they were still not prepared to compromise.

TWENTY

IT'S YOUR ERA NOW

t seemed that fans in the US, UK and Australia would have to wait a while for an English-language BTS track, but the Japanese editions were proving to be a Big Hit masterstroke. 'Chi, Ase, Namida', the Japanese version of 'Blood, Sweat & Tears', was released in May 2017 with a new music video, a vividly coloured and at times psychedelic alternative to the Korean original. The track immediately matched 'For You' by going to the top of Japan's Billboard Hot 100 and the Oricon charts. Not a bad start for the group on their new record label in Japan, the legendary hip-hop label Def Jam, now home to Justin Bieber and Kanye West among others.

Between the end of May and early July the boys played thirteen *Wings* concerts to around 145,000 fans across Japan. BTS were breaking new Japanese records for foreign group sales and their name was becoming familiar to more and more people there. They even made their first appearance on a Japanese variety show, *Sukkiri*, where they showed off their Japanese language skills and performed 'Chi, Ase, Namida'.

While on tour, they were also welcomed to the famous Koshien Stadium to watch the Hanshin Tigers play the Nippon-Han Fighters at baseball. Apart from J-Hope, who had his lucky '7', and Jimin with his birth date '13', the boys sported Tigers baseball shirts with their birth year as a number and Jungkook was chosen to deliver the ceremonial first pitch in front of a packed stadium. The Golden *Maknae* proceeded to add baseball to his many talents as, to the delight of the watching members, he delivered a pretty decent throw. That's Jungkook, some said: always pitch-perfect!

That's Jungkook ... always pitch-perfect!

They might have been in Japan, but there was no way BTS were going to forget their *festa*. June 2017 marked their fourth anniversary and, just as on the previous three, they aimed to celebrate with their beloved ARMY. Celebrations got underway with a collection of pictures from the year in a Facebook photobook, Jungkook and Jimin's now-cherished cover of Charlie Puth and Selena Gomez's 'We Don't Talk Anymore' and the YouTube release of two special 'choreography stages': the dance practice videos of 'Not Today', using a gymnasium rather than the usual dance studio to accommodate all the supporting dancers, and 'I Like It Pt. 2'. Then a surprise! They dropped a great new video of them filming themselves performing live in Sydney, so we see not only the group's view of ARMY in full voice, but also close-ups of them having a great time on stage and really playing up to the camera.

The traditional family photos provided the usual fun, including a hilarious update on their school uniforms-and-shades pic from 2014 (cue the 'haven't they grown up!' squeals).

The climax of the *festa* was their 'home party' back in Korea, when they held an intimate celebration at the Woori Art Hall in the Olympic Park in Seoul. The thousand tickets were sold only to those who had recently joined the fan club, although the show was also shown live (and is still available with English subtitles) on V-Live.

After a genuinely funny filmed intro in which they re-enacted the 'Blood, Sweat & Tears' video in their dorm, the guys teamed up according to their dorm rooms: team R&V (RM and V), team 3J (J-Hope, Jimin and Jungkook) and team Sin (Jin and Suga). Throughout the show they played games, took part in quizzes on their roommates and gave team performances. Team R&V performed a self-composed song, '4 O'Clock', live for the first time; team 3J covered various urban dance choreographies; and team Sin's contribution was Jin rapping Suga's 'Nevermind' and Suga singing 'Awake'. Finally, after revealing particularly cute baby pictures of each of them, the audience was treated to a funny kindergarten medley of some of their hits.

BANGTAN BOMB

613 BTS HOME PARTY PRACTICE – UNIT STAGE

A longer than usual Bangtan bomb, this series of clips shows team 3J from the home party practising their moves for the *festa* extravaganza. While it can't help but make you smile to see them enjoying themselves, it also gives an insight into how hard they work at getting the choreography spot on – and just how much they love to dance, whether it's in the dance studio, backstage at the 2017 Billboard Music Awards or in J-Hope's hotel room (with Jimin practising in his dressing gown and a face pack!).

In the summer of 2017 a second series of *Bon Voyage* appeared on the V-Live channel and this time the trip was to their dream destination, Hawaii. The boys duly don their Hawaiian shirts and straw hats and, over eight episodes, we see them having fun together, playing hide-and-seek around the hotel, snorkelling and stargazing after watching an amazing sunset.

There are none of the Nordic trip's trials and tribulations, but they are forced to be self-sufficient when it comes to ordering their individual meals at Ken's House of Pancakes, although Jimin 'somehow' manages to attract help from a waitress, and, split into teams, they are tasked with finding their way to their lodge on Oahu. There the adrenaline-rush adventures really start as they take a helicopter ride over the active volcano – with Suga sitting right by the open door! – and swim in an underwater cage right next to a school of sharks.

There's still fun to be had before they go back to idol life. They really enjoy tearing along the coastal road on quad bikes and, at a Polynesian-themed evening, J-Hope, Jimin and V are invited to the stage for some Bangtan Hawaiian dance, all in perfect synchronicity of course. The final episode sees them taking a boat ride. V is delighted when the skipper gives him the wheel, but as he piles on the speed, the others seem rather alarmed.

Fortunately, it all calms down for the finale. Each of them has written a letter to one of the others and, as they recall when they first met and reveal what they mean to each other, it's very emotional. The letter that really melts hearts is V's letter to Jimin, in which he describes how much his 95-line friend has helped him through the years. Most ARMY must watch the final dance party on the boat through tear-filled eyes.

While the *festa* had given BTS an opportunity to repay their fans for the love and support that had made them idols, soon they were able to repay a debt of a different kind when they were invited to participate in the twenty-fifth anniversary celebrations of Seo Taiji and Boys, the group that had launched the whole K-pop phenomenon. In 1992 their rap-rock track 'I Know' entered the Korean charts alongside the traditional *trot* numbers and ballads. It went on to the top of the charts and stayed there for seventeen weeks. Nothing would ever be the same again. Not only was their sound different, but they also sang challenging lyrics that reflected the frustrations of young people. Now who does that remind you of?

The Boys, Yang Hyun-suk and Lee Juno, had left in 1996 (Yang Hyun-suk starting major company YG Entertainment), but over the next two decades Seo Taiji had continued to push musical boundaries and now he was receiving his recognition as the godfather of K-pop, with an album, *Time Traveler*, featuring remakes of his songs and a special concert in Seoul. BTS were the honoured guests for both.

For the album, BTS revisited the 1995 classic 'Come Back Home'. A dark and gritty rap song, the original spoke of the pressures that made so many Korean teenagers run away from home, so it felt just right when BTS, in a style that harked back to 'No More Dream' and 'N.O', injected their own rap parts and some Bangtan lyrical magic, including a Jin falsetto opening, in an invigorating reworking of the song.

On 3 September 2017, in front of 35,000 fans at the Olympic Stadium, Taiji, often nicknamed the 'President of Culture' in South Korea, went through his impressive collection of hits. In place of the Boys were BTS, taking it in turns to serve as back-up vocalists and dancers for their hero. At rehearsals they addressed him

> Taiji acknowledged the achievements of BTS and pronounced them his successors by declaring, 'It's your era now.'

as 'Father', but the respect went both ways. In a break in the concert, Taiji acknowledged the achievements of BTS and pronounced them his successors by declaring, 'It's your era now.'

If this signified that BTS led the current generation of K-pop acts, then their summer change of logo and name reflected their position as a global force. They would still be BTS, but in English that would now stand for 'Beyond the Scene' – a new way of presenting themselves to the English-speaking world. At the same time, they issued new and complementary logos for BTS and for ARMY. These were pairs of simple but stylish quadrilaterals representing doors; the doors which youth pass through to adulthood. Both the group and ARMY were now ready for a new chapter in BTS's journey.

Back in May, at the 2017 Billboard Music Awards in the States, RM had announced in his acceptance speech: 'Please, ARMY, remember what we say: "Love myself, love yourself."' That phrase came to mind again three months later as the *Love Yourself* comeback got underway. It started with posters of each of the group, the first of which shocked ARMY by showing Jungkook in a wheelchair. Each poster was accompanied by a short statement giving a downbeat and personal notion of love, such as 'I lied, because there's no reason to love someone like me' or 'Don't come closer, it will only make you unhappy.' A further set of posters paired the members up in light and dark photos, although, as always, Jin was alone.

The four short videos (now available as a thirteen-minute highlight reel) that subsequently appeared, built on these images. As in previous films, they were loaded with symbolism and references to previous stories and, although these sparked an outpouring of online analysis from ARMY, they also contained a narrative that can simply be enjoyed. They feature each of the group looking like a boy next door (albeit a boy next door with a floppy fringe, stylish casual clothes and a to-die-for complexion) in a troubled romantic situation. Apart from J-Hope and Jimin, each is attracted to a different woman, but as the stories unfold, self-doubt, shyness, jealousy, frustration and even tragedy are shown to thwart the course of true love. And, for those who are still concerned, Jungkook does get back on his feet – eventually.

The mini-album *Love Yourself: Her* was set to appear in four versions, *L*, *O*, *V* and *E*, and so four separate photo collections were released. There are no smoky eyes or remarkable hairstyles this time. The look is natural, the haircuts similar. Jimin, Jin, V and Jungkook go for subtle colours and J-Hope gets most attention with a colour fans call 'pumpkin spice'.

In the photos for *L* and *O* the guys wear subdued colours and the shots are dreamy and relaxing, while those for *V* and *E* are more vibrant and they are in colourful casual sportswear. Meanwhile, the trailer featured a similarly dreamy Jimin (a yellow-blond Jimin!) solo in a setting that combined a dazzling white room with oceans and galaxies. In an article in *Vogue* magazine, Suga explained, 'It's about boys falling in love. There are four versions of love and we shot four different photos to show them. Though each one is different, the same feeling of love comes through in every shot. There's a sense of playfulness, of friends hanging out comfortably at home in their free time, and that kind of fluttering feeling.'

It was the colourful look (plus a lot of stonewash and Jimin's fabulous Gucci sequin bomber jacket) that drove the dance-focused video for the lead track, 'DNA'. The boys are in an array of colours against a kaleidoscope of backgrounds that change from cheesy retro computer style to candy stripes, swirls, deep space, geometric patterns and sometimes neon.

The cameras couldn't keep pace with their footwork.

Their choreography was pretty stunning: controlled, at times intricate, and interspersed with a series of stunningly fast moves. *Billboard* reported that when they performed it at the American Music Awards (AMAs) on 19 November the cameras couldn't keep pace with their footwork. Some claimed it was the most difficult set of steps yet and on a V-Live appearance V joked, 'We mastered the difficult choreography after practising for more than four hours, but J-Hope finished it in ten minutes.'

In their press conferences and interviews it became clear that BTS viewed *Love Yourself: Her* as the beginning of a new era. RM referred to it as the 'second chapter' of the group and left a message on the fan café saying it would be a turning point for BTS. It was an extremely confident album and stylistically wide-ranging as they assimilated guest contributors alongside their usual producers. As billed, they portray the exhilarating, ecstatic but also uneasy feelings of young adults who fall in love, but they also use gender-neutral lyrics for the first time, acknowledge and even tease their fans, and include a track aimed directly at their own generation.

BTS viewed *Love Yourself: Her* as the beginning of a new era.

When the album was released on 18 September 2017, the opener was, of course, familiar from the teaser. It was the first time a vocalist had been trusted with the task and the privilege fell to Jimin. He delivers 'Serendipity', described as a 'chill-out-style urban song', with delicate ease, singing of a perfect predestined love. It is a theme that's carried over to the lead track 'DNA'. Jungkook's catchy whistled opener is still lingering as the song begins in earnest with a unique acoustic guitar-based EDM track and a breakdown of the usual distinct rap and vocal lines.

At the Billboard Awards, The Chainsmokers had shared a photo of themselves with BTS with the caption, 'Love these dudes.' When the US band played in Korea, BTS joined them on stage to perform 'Closer' and now a collaboration between the two groups appeared on the album. 'Best of Me' is classic electronic dance music: anthemic with a catchy chorus and totally uplifting.

The next track, 'Dimple', uses the tune of Allison Kaplan's 'Illegal' and the lyrics were written by the guy with the most talked-about dimples in BTS – RM – but he sits out as the vocal line, especially Jin, makes it sweet and sensual. This takes us on to 'Pied Piper', an ode to their fans – or is it? *Billboard*'s Tamar Herman claimed it was 'BTS's most subversive song of their career, thanks to its takedown of the very fan culture that has helped the act thrive'. Over the mellow disco number the group mercilessly tease ARMY everywhere by explaining what a terrible distraction they are from school work and other important aspects of life, but, at the same time, openly relishing and celebrating their irresistibility.

'Skit: Billboard Music Awards Speech' isn't actually a skit; it's a recording of BTS's historic triumph at the previous year's BBMAs, from the winning announcement and the cheers of the fans to RM's acceptance speech and ending with feedback that takes us into 'MIC Drop'. Here the rap line returns in force with a song inspired by President Obama's 'OK, I'm done' mic drop at his final White House Correspondents' dinner. The pretend-apologetic bragging (sorry we aren't the failures you predicted) rap is an update on the old Bangtan sound enhanced by a chorus that hangs around in your head.

Have BTS forgotten their social conscience? Of course not. The next track, 'Go Go', proves that. It might have a trendy tropical-influenced soft disco sound, but the lyrics hit hard. In contrast to the music, the words are angry and defiant, condemning society for leaving a young generation bereft of ambition and expectations to seek thrills through a YOLO (you only live once), spend now, worry later lifestyle.

The album closes with 'Outro: Her', where, over a lush, laid-back instrumental, the rap line sounds so chilled they're virtually singing. There is no switching of the mic, just an extended verse for each of the three to display their own style and explain their notion of the uncertainties of being in love. And there, after thirty minutes of diverse BTS styles as the group forge new ideas, sounds and paths, the album ends.

The physical album treated buyers to two more 'hidden' tracks, which BTS felt didn't fit the 'love' concept but deserved inclusion. 'Skit: Hesitation and Fear' is one of their most revealing conversations and is worth reading in translation. You'll discover how scared they were that they might never debut, how they never took English or Japanese lessons seriously, and how anxious they are about coping with their success. The track 'Sea', mainly written and produced by RM, takes up some of these themes in an old-style BTS rap and vocal track based around the refrain 'Where there is hope, there are trials.' And that really is the end this time.

On 21 September 2017, BTS had their official comeback show with a live broadcast in which they performed 'MIC Drop', 'Go Go' and 'DNA' from the album, as well as 'I Need U' and 'No More Dream'. It featured the guys talking about the album along with some fun films of them at home and their recollections of the early days of BTS, including re-enactments of their auditions.

At home, *Love Yourself: Her* reached new heights. It debuted at

BANGTAN BOMB

GO (GO GO) DANCE PRACTICE (HALLOWEEN VER.)

This 2017 Halloween special where Snow White and the six dwarfs perform 'Go Go' is the most popular Bangtan bomb ever with over 50 million views. That's no surprise because it's fabulously executed. From the moment the rock, paper, scissors game lands V in the dress, he steals the show with a magnificent deadpan performance, complete with poisoned apple, but his laughing dwarfs offer spot-on support.

number one in Korea on the Gaon album chart and became the biggest-selling physical album for sixteen years, every song from the album featured in the Melon chart top ten and it swept the board at the music shows. 'DNA' brought them another ten show awards, including their first triple crowns (three consecutive weeks) on *Music Bank* and *Inkigayo*.

BTS finished the comeback with another special broadcast. With Jin acting as MC, *BTS Countdown!* was a parody of *M Countdown*, with a chart show, music stages, a mini drama and game segments – but all starring BTS. It included a segment where they danced to 'Boy in Luv' using only the bottom half of their bodies, a slo-mo 'Fire' choreography and a punishment finale where the losing team – V, J-Hope and Jimin – had to dance at double speed to the song voted their best ever: 'DNA'.

Love Yourself: Her was never going to flop. The million-plus pre-orders guaranteed that – but its success was perhaps even beyond their wildest hopes. On the day it was released the album immediately sailed to number one in the iTunes Top Albums Chart in over seventy countries. It reached number one in Japan in its second week, opened at number seven on the Billboard 200 and, for the first time ever, hit the UK Top 40 album chart, peaking at fourteen. Meanwhile, it was trending at number one on YouTube, an achievement unheard of for a K-pop group.

TWENTY-ONE

HEART AND SEOUL

With the comeback completed, BTS had a chance to spend time on some projects close to their hearts. Chief among these was a desire to support #ENDViolence, a campaign by the international children's charity UNICEF to stop children and teenagers having to live in fear of violence. Along with Big Hit, they sponsored the hashtag, giving nearly $350,000 to the campaign and pledging 3 per cent of sales income from all the physical albums in the *Love Yourself* series.

Next on the to-do list was a present for the city they had made their home, the South Korean capital, Seoul. To support the city's tourism department, they dropped a free track called 'With Seoul', a cheery orchestrated pop hymn to the city sung by the vocal line. The video, which featured the whole group recording the song cut with the city's sights, was released on the official tourist website, which immediately crashed as fans attempted to watch it.

BTS also found time to get creative with their pens. No strangers to caricature versions of themselves, BTS had already seen the Hip Hip Monsters and the We On superheroes. Now Japanese messaging app, Line, gave them an opportunity to draw characters for an emoji sticker set. They came up with a set of seven adorable friends: the kind, parkawearing alpaca, RJ (Jin); the eager-to-please puppy Chimmy (Jimin); a magic cookie named Shooky who is scared of milk (Suga); a dancing masked pony, Mang (J-Hope); the super-curious heart-faced Tata (V); Cooky the wannabe tough-guy bunny (Jungkook); and Koya, the thoughtful if sleepy koala (RM). They even came up with a character for ARMY, the friends' space robot protector named Van. If you don't find them all unbearably cute, there's no hope for you.

In December, BTS themselves were given a present: a new dorm. Well, it was more a luxury apartment than a dorm, as they moved into Hannam The Hill, the most select and expensive block in Seoul. Although many idol groups choose to live apart when they become successful, BTS are very close and opted to stay together, although at least they each had their own room here.

Although many idol groups choose to live apart when they become successful, BTS are very close and opted to stay together.

Not that they had much time to settle in, as they were off to the US again, because they had been asked to perform at the 2017 AMAs, which was a real coup – they were the first Korean group to receive such an invitation. Could they wow the US audience with 'DNA', singing in Korean? In their first major televised stateside performance? Actually, as they say in the US, they had them at hello.

Style authority *Vogue* declared that BTS 'shut down' the red carpet in their sleek black suits, courtesy of Saint Laurent designer Anthony Vaccarello. 'Standing together,' *Vogue* swooned, 'they reinforced their message of shared style with a personal twist. It won't be the last time we see it.' Before they even made the stage, the boys were caught on camera dancing in their seats and mouthing all the words to Demi Lovato's

'Sorry Not Sorry', but no one (except the thousands of ARMY around the world) knew what was about to unfold when The Chainsmokers introduced these seven incredible-looking guys in their 'DNA' outfits of jeans and assorted Gucci jackets.

The knife-like choreography was totally on point, the synchronization exact and they played to the audience, including viewers watching at home, perfectly. In short, their performance was immaculate, but even so the reaction stunned everyone. Led by a screaming ARMY contingent, the crowd, celebs included, gave them a standing ovation. 'I need a moment to recover from that performance,' said presenter Jared Leto immediately afterwards. He wasn't alone.

> Their performance [at the 2017 AMAs] was immaculate.

The post-event reaction was also incredible. Twitter caught fire with ARMY and brand-new fans raving about their performance in over 20 million tweets. 'All anyone cared about at the AMAs was South Korean boy band BTS', was the *Mashable* headline. And this on a night when Shawn Mendes, Selena Gomez and Christina Aguilera had also performed. BTS could have hung out with those guys had they attended the star-studded after-show party. Why weren't they there? Simply because they wanted to share their first offstage moment with their fans. In a live broadcast from their hotel room, they talked about their performance, how Suga had been so nervous his mic was shaking and how several stars – Jin is shushed when he mentions Zedd – had offered to collaborate with them.

One American, however, had beaten those stars to it. Legendary DJ and producer Steve Aoki had remixed 'MIC Drop' for the US market and the result was about to be unleashed. The remix transformed the song into a full-on rap track, as Aoki overlaid an EDM beat, introduced

English-language verses and brought in US rapper Desiigner. The track has a great music video, with the boys in both old-style BTS hip-hop black and white and their colourful new look. It features Aoki masterminding the track as BTS break free from an interrogation room and take on their black-hooded haters. Exciting stuff.

Having 'discovered' BTS, US television wanted more. ARMY packed the audience at *The Ellen DeGeneres Show*, with the host making comparisons to the reception the Beatles had received in America in the 1960s. With the help of an on-set interpreter, Ellen asked about the 'social conscience' messages of their songs and even dared ask if they had 'hooked up' with any ARMY. When they figured out what she meant, the completely shocked reaction of the guys was an answer in itself. On the show, they performed the new version of 'MIC Drop', which probably helped them become the first K-pop act to hit number one on the US iTunes charts.

Before the AMAs, they recorded a mini-concert for *Jimmy Kimmel Live!* – in front of a passionate crowd of around a thousand fans in Los Angeles, they played 'Go Go', 'Save Me', 'I Need U', 'Fire' and 'MIC Drop (Remix)', which was played on the show itself (the full concert was uploaded to Kimmel's YouTube channel). In a short segment on the late-night show, Kimmel introduced BTS, explaining how many of their passionate ARMY had waited in line for the show. The clip then showed some of the fans' mothers being taken out of the queue and into the studio. They FaceTimed their so-jealous daughters as they met the boys. This trick was only appreciated by their girls when they were eventually taken to meet the group too!

More fun and games awaited them on *The Late Late Show with James Corden*. Before performing 'DNA', the group were persuaded to play Corden's game of 'Flinch', where they stood behind a plexiglass wall and tried not to flinch as Corden fired fruit at them from a high-pressure air cannon. Jin and J-Hope, described by RM as the biggest cowards of the group, went first and proved their leader right by freaking out (Jin) and collapsing hilariously (J-Hope). Although Jimin, Suga and RM, the last three to step up, acted pretty brave, they still recoiled, leaving the unflappable V and pretty cool Jungkook as winners. It's fun stuff and worth searching for online.

BTS brought an unforgettable year to a close when, in December 2017, they stepped out at the Gocheok Sky Dome in Seoul for the final performances of a *Wings* world tour that had seen them play thirty-two concerts in ten different countries. It was a triumphant return, a thrilling three-hour-long love-in between BTS and ARMY which the *Korea Herald* described as 'tearful, beautiful and splendid'. This was not only the end of a long tour, but the finale of a trilogy that had begun back in 2014 at a time when many had still doubted them.

More than ever, New Year was a time for celebration. The recently released Japanese single, 'Crystal Snow', a beautiful and emotional ballad adorned with Jin's soulful high vocals, had not only reached number one in the Japanese charts, but had registered high on iTunes charts around the world. Meanwhile, back in the US, the group's profile remained high, with pre-recorded performances of 'MIC Drop' and 'DNA' appearing on the iconic TV show *Dick Clark's New Year's Rockin' Eve with Ryan Seacrest*.

As the awards season got underway, millions around the world followed BTS's progress and expectations were high. They would not be disappointed. They picked up *daesangs* at MAMA (Artist of the Year for two years running!), MMA (Song of the Year and Global Artist prizes), won their first Golden Disc Awards *daesang* for *Love Yourself: Her*, Seoul Music Awards *daesang* for Artist of the Year and,

BTS became the first idol group to win the Korean Music Awards' Artist of the Year.

perhaps most impressively, became the first idol group to win the Korean Music Awards' Artist of the Year, a prestigious honour bestowed by critics and music professionals.

Early spring was a strange time and fans waited impatiently for news. Surely the next *Love Yourself* instalment was due? Were rumours of a global tour true? Would BTS be returning to the US for the Billboard Music Awards? Answers to these questions were not forthcoming, but on 1 March there was nonetheless something to get excited about in the form of J-Hope's mixtape, *Hope World*. This had been talked about for so long that ARMY had almost given up on it ever appearing, but it was worth the wait. A superb collection of upbeat, positive tracks that only BTS's very own ray of sunshine could supply, within hours of its release *Hope World* topped iTunes album charts in over sixty countries and J-Hope's music video for the lead song, 'Daydream', amassed 12 million YouTube views in its first twenty-four hours.

YouTube had long been an integral part of the BTS success story, so it was fitting that the new fly-on-the-wall documentary *Burn the Stage* was shown exclusively on the site (the first two episodes are free-to-view with the rest part of the YouTube Red paid-for service). The series, taking a behind-the-scenes look at the group's 2017 *Wings* tour, makes for compelling viewing. As a group that have always been open and honest, they don't hold back, and allow the cameras to see their self-doubt, their fears and their arguments, as well as the elation, the fun, and the love and respect they have for each other.

It is not short of drama, with Jungkook collapsing from heat exhaustion and a heated and emotional row between V and Jin over their onstage positioning, as well as fun moments like Jungkook sneaking a chocolate ball into Jin's noodles and Jin thinking it's a mushroom. But what is most amazing is that all we have learned about BTS is true: they do work until they collapse, they do care for each other and they are involved in every aspect of their performance, from the music to the stage production. And if you think their words aren't heartfelt, these films show how much they appreciate the love and how they feel the burden of repaying the loyalty of ARMY.

> These films show how much they appreciate the love and how they feel the burden of repaying the loyalty of ARMY.

The series played out to a flurry of BTS action. At the start of April, electronics company LG announced a new association with the group. So far, so dull. However, the accompanying photo caused ARMY to do a double-take. Yes, there were all seven boys with dark hair, for the first time ever! No wonder #BTSBlackHairParty was trending worldwide on Twitter. Two days later, a twelve-track Japanese album, *Face Yourself*, was released. It wasn't the album they were waiting for, but ARMY did at least have some new BTS music to enjoy. Along with Japanese versions of 'Blood, Sweat & Tears', 'DNA' and 'MIC Drop', there were new intro and outro tracks and two previously unheard songs: 'Don't Leave Me' and 'Let Go'.

'Don't Leave Me' is a powerful and emotional EDM-based song that finally puts Jin centre-stage. He shows he deserves it by sending down some jaw-dropping soprano lines. 'Let Go', a sentimental ballad that swells and falls then rises again, is especially notable for Jimin's pretty perfect English singing. The album, of course, was a number-one hit in Japan, but BTS fans now had such an appetite for new material that it charted all around the world.

On 5 April BTS appeared in a video on DreamStillLives.com, a project to honour civil rights activist Dr Martin Luther King Jr, who had been assassinated exactly fifty years previously. The group were personally invited to contribute by the organizer, US soul legend Stevie Wonder, along with such famous faces as Barack and Michelle Obama, Mariah Carey, Meryl Streep and Elton John.

That same day saw the release of a nine-minute video titled 'Euphoria: Theme of Love Yourself Wonder'. Did this herald the long-awaited album? Many thought it did. A dramatic introduction featured clips from previous videos set to classical composer Debussy's piece 'Clair de Lune'. Then there was a sudden change and Jungkook's dreamy solo vocals rose over a bright synth-pop backing and an alternative scenario was played out where the boys, dressed in colourful but plain clothes, were having fun together once more. Finally, the end section found them all in white at the water's edge where V jumped from the pier in the 'On Stage: Prologue' video. Once again there were more questions than answers, but ARMY didn't mind. If you're up to some theorizing, it might help to know that the message in the final frame translates as: '*Hyung* is that all?'

Fans had two weeks to puzzle it all out before the new album was announced. To great surprise, it was to be called *Love Yourself: Tear* and not *Wonder* as many had assumed. The comeback trailer, 'Singularity', uploaded to YouTube on 6 May, featured V performing solo. The elegant RM-penned R&B track, with music from British producer Charlie J. Perry, was superbly complemented by a captivating video in which V dances alone or with backing dancers to lush backdrops or a recurring mask motif. It was just one member, but enough to convince ARMY that something momentous was about to drop.

The concept photos only served to heighten the excitement. Once again there would be four versions, this time spelling *Y, O, U* and *R*, although the pictures weren't released in that order. Seven boys in smart double-denim rocked the *R* version; dreamy black-and-white snaps made up the *O* shoot; the *Y* version showed the members posing against a blue sky in heightened colours; and the *U* version went for the unified white look seen at the end of the 'Euphoria' video. As people waited for the album to come out, the talk was all about the lead track, 'Fake Love', which they would perform for the first time at the BBMAs. BTS were once again nominated for the top social artist award and few bet against them taking it home.

For ARMY it seemed to take ages, but 18 May came around – eventually. The CD box was a reverse of *Love Yourself: Her*; just the title in white on a black background. It included the usual extensive photo book and photo cards, but also a twenty-page mini-book of 'notes' with more diary-style stories from each of the members. The CD itself contained eleven new tracks, introduced by V's trailer 'Singularity'. The boys themselves were already in the US on release day, but the magic of V-Live allowed them to broadcast their preview show to over 3 million viewers.

BTS promoted the album widely, but no interview was loved as much as Buzzfeed's YouTube video 'BTS Plays with Puppies While Answering Fan Questions'. Not a lot of information was gleaned but hey, puppies and Bangtan Boys: what's not to like? More informative, if a lot less cute, was RM's interview with *J-14* magazine's Liam McEwan. He neatly outlined the theme of *Love Yourself: Tear*, saying, 'Basically love is complex. There's sort of some sides that make us really feel bad or depressed. There could be tears, there could be sadness. So this time we wanted to focus on some of the parts of love that we want to run away from. So the name is *Tear*.'

The second and lead track, 'Fake Love', picks up this idea and is a breathless combination of epic beats, rap rock, lush vocals and serious harmonies tied together with the catchiest of choruses. Meanwhile the video utilizes many BTS trademark styles, bringing in contemporary dance and sharp, synchronized moves; amazing settings full of explosions, flames and floods; desperate running; and lingering shots. It was devoured by fans as soon as it dropped, #FakeLoveFRIDAY soon trended on Twitter and it racked up 4.8 million views in its first hour.

> #FakeLoveFRIDAY soon trended on Twitter and it racked up 4.8 million views in its first hour.

The album itself is a triumph of genre-hopping. The boys effortlessly move from the tender piano-accompanied ballad of 'The Truth Untold', written and produced by Steve Aoki of 'MIC Drop' fame, to the flutes and jazzy guitar of '134340', which takes the dwarf planet Pluto as a metaphor for lost love, and on to the rap-fuelled 'Paradise', another great BTS message song in which they reassure their generation that they can just enjoy the moment and ignore the burden of their dreams and ambitions. The beautiful harmonies of 'Love Maze', with traces of BTS 2013-style rap, complete the first half of the album.

The second half seems to be gift-wrapped for ARMY. 'Magic Shop', written by Jungkook (his first ever credit), offers fans strength and escape with BTS, and 'Airplane Pt. 2', a sequel to the popular track from J-Hope's mixtape, is a trippy feast with a fabulous Spanish feel (perhaps influenced by the success of 'Despacito'). The next two tracks, destined to be fan favourites, are 'Anpanman' (the name of a Japanese comic book superhero), three minutes of pure fun with great singalong and dance-along potential, and 'So What', the kind of up-tempo anthemic dance track which brings ARMY and BTS together at concerts. Finally comes the outro, but there's no sweet-tongued ballad here, as the rap line spit out an angry and bitter break-up song as a defiant end to the album. There was no doubt: the Bangtan Boys had done it again.

As the group prepared for the Billboard Music Awards in Las Vegas, *Love Yourself: Tear* and 'Fake Love' stood at the top of iTunes charts in over sixty different countries. Around the world, in every time zone, fans watched them walk the magenta carpet in a live feed on Twitter. They appeared looking chilled and cool in seven different Gucci outfits, including RM in shades and Hawaiian shirt, Jin smart in a waistcoat and tie, and J-Hope in a piped school blazer and yellow T-shirt. They strolled across the carpet as if they owned the place.

'Fake Love' stood at the top of iTunes charts in over sixty different countries.

They charmed the watching audience, sending a message to their fans in Korea and revealing their 'no tweeting when drunk' rule. They hung out backstage meeting old and making new celebrity friends, including Taylor Swift, Lil Pump, Pharrell Williams and John Legend, and, of course, they won the top social artist award – again. In his acceptance speech, RM dedicated the award to ARMY, saying, 'This time we had a chance to think about what "social" really means for us. And some of our fans told us that our music really changed their lives. And now we realize that our words truly carry weight thanks to you guys.'

A few days later, the guys were back on screen with a visit to their old friend Ellen DeGeneres. In front of another hyped-up audience, RM told Ellen that she was personally responsible for teaching the whole of South Korea the meaning of the word 'hook-up' after her

BANGTAN BOMB

'FAKE LOVE' LIVE PERFORMANCE @2018

In front of an already screaming audience at the BBMAs, the seven members perform 'Fake Love', their choreography, devised by Tokyo-based Rie Hata, creating a cascade of shapes, patterns, waves and synchronized movement ending in a perfectly timed and graceful group hug. The crowd went wild, celebrities, from Tyra Banks and Rebel Wilson to the Backstreet Boys, flocked to get pictures with them, and the internet nearly broke.

presumptuous question in their previous meeting. When Ellen again asked if any band members had a girlfriend, most of the audience screamed 'pick me!' However, the 'fangirl' who jumped out at them on stage was a male stagehand in a wig, a prepared prank by the production team.

It was time once again to return to Seoul, but they wouldn't be home long as a new world tour was set for the autumn. First the tour would cross Canada and the USA, with the fourteen dates selling out instantly. Then, for the first time, they would tour Europe. ARMY across the continent had been pleading to see the boys perform live and now Big Hit had answered their prayers. Two concerts at London's O2 Arena, which sold out in mere minutes, would be followed by shows in Amsterdam, Berlin and Paris. Were the European ARMY ready for them? Oh yes!

On 27 May 2018, the weekly Billboard 200 charts were announced.

Love Yourself: Tear was the number-one album in the USA and BTS were the first K-pop group ever to achieve that feat. Almost five years since their debut, they had accomplished the unthinkable: BTS had conquered the world.

GLOSSARY

K-pop has its own distinct culture and vocabulary, so you might find some of the words and concepts unfamiliar. The following is a reference to some of the Korean and K-pop-specific words used in the book.

4D: A K-pop description of someone who is quirky or eccentric. Intended as a compliment.

Aegyo: A display of cuteness through facial expressions or body language.

Ahjae **joke:** A terrible joke or pun, a 'dad joke'.

All-kill: When a song simultaneously goes to number one in a number of charts, usually immediately after release.

ARMY: The official name given to BTS fans, standing for 'Adorable Representative MC for Youth'.

Bias: A personal favourite of a group.

Bias wrecker: A group member who does something (good) to question or change your bias.

Big Three: The three biggest, most successful and dominant entertainment companies in K-pop: YG Entertainment, SM Entertainment and JYP Entertainment.

Bonsang: A prize given to up to twelve different acts at an award ceremony (less prestigious than a *daesang*).

Chocolate abs: Defined, abdominal muscles that resemble the subdivided parts of a chocolate bar – also known as a six-pack.

Comeback: When an artist releases a new single, mini-album, or album and promotes them with TV broadcasts or performances.

Daebak: A word to describe a great success or something awesome, or an exclamation similar to 'wow!'

Daesang: The prestigious 'Grand Prize' at a Music Awards, awarded for artist, song or album of the year.

Debut: An act's first performance (usually on TV). The official launch of an act is a crucial opportunity to make an impression on the watching public.

Fandom: Short for 'fan domain', it includes everything that goes on in the fan community, from fan clubs to online forums.

Festa: A festival or celebration.

Gayo: Any kind of pop music.

Hallyu: Refers to 'The Korean Wave', a growing interest in South Korean culture that has spread worldwide in the twenty-first century.

Hwaiting!: An exclamation of support and encouragement similar to sports fans' cries of 'Come on!' – it translates as 'Fighting!'

Hyung: A Korean mark of respect spoken by a man to a close, usually older, male friend or brother. It can stand alongside or be used in conjunction with the name, such as 'Namjoon-hyung'.

Idol: An artist in mainstream and commercial K-pop.

Line: A word used to link together group members or friends. Often used with a year (e.g. 95 line) to group individuals born in that year or with a group designation such as 'rap line' or 'vocal line'.

Maknae: The youngest member; as such they are allowed to be silly or mischievous and are expected to be cute.

Mini-album: An album containing four to six songs.

MV: Abbreviation for 'Music Video', usually uploaded on YouTube.

Noona: The name a man gives to an older female.

Rookie: A group who has debuted but is still in their first – or sometimes, second – year.

Satoori: Korean word for 'regional dialect'.

Selca: A selfie.

Single album: Like an EP with a lead song and one or two other songs.

Stan: A passionate fan. Also used as a verb, as in 'You should stan Jimin.'

Teaser: Photos, messages and short videos put out before the release of a single, album or concert.

Trainee: A young performer signed to an entertainment company in order to train in dance, singing and other performing arts with a view to becoming an idol.

Underground: Non-commercial focused acts who work outside the mainstream. Comparable with the English music term 'indie'.

Visual: The group member who is considered the most beautiful or a member who is included in the group because of their looks.

ACKNOWLEDGEMENTS

I would like to thank Louise Dixon at Michael O'Mara Books for initiating the project, George Maudsley and Becca Wright for their invaluable editorial advice and assistance as well as Becca for recognizing the potential of this book and providing many informed observations, and Nick Fawcett for copy-editing. I am also incredibly grateful to Lisa Hughes and Nora Besley for their willingness to endlessly discuss BTS and read through drafts. Finally, I would like to acknowledge the work of ARMY around the world, whose dedication to recording, translating and writing about every aspect of BTS and K-pop have helped me enormously.

PICTURE CREDITS

Page 1: Han Myung-Gu / WireImage / Getty Images (top); ilgan Sports / Multi-Bits via Getty Images (bottom)

Page 2: Frazer Harrison / Getty Images (top left, top right, bottom right); Jeff Kravitz / FilmMagic / Getty Images (bottom left)

Page 3: Frazer Harrison / Getty Images (top and bottom); Kevin Mazur / WireImage / Getty Images (centre)

Page 4: Han Myung-Gu / WireImage / Getty Images (both)

Page 5: Han Myung-Gu / WireImage / Getty Images (top); Paul Zimmerman / Getty Images (bottom)

Page 6: John Shearer / Getty Images (top); TPG / Zuma Press / PA Images (bottom)

Page 7: RB / Bauer-Griffin / GC Images / Getty Images (top); Lionel Hahn / ABACA / PA Images (bottom)

Page 8: Frank Micelotta / PictureGroup / SIPA USA / PA Images

Page 9: Frank Micelotta / PictureGroup / SIPA USA / PA Images (top left); Jeff Kravitz / FilmMagic / Getty Images (top right); REX / Shutterstock (bottom left); Yonhap / Yonhap News Agency / PA Images (bottom right)

Page 10: Yonhap / Yonhap News Agency / PA Images (top); Santiago Felipe / Getty Images (bottom)

Page 11: Yonhap / Yonhap News Agency / PA Images (both)

Pages 12-13: Yonhap / Yonhap News Agency / PA Images

Page 14: John Salangsang / BFA / REX / Shutterstock (top); Kevin Mazure / WireImage / Getty Images (bottom)

Page 15: Ethan Miller / Getty Images (top); Kevin Mazur / BBMA18 / WireImage (bottom)

Page 16: Yonhap / Yonhap News Agency / PA Images (top); Terence Patrick / CBS via Getty Images (bottom)

INDEX

(Page numbers in **bold** indicate main entries for
BTS band members and ARMY)